P9-DCV-355

FaceTime

BIBLE ANSWERS TO **TEENS' TOUGHEST** QUESTIONS

To order additional copies of *Face Time,* by the General Conference
Youth Ministries Department, call 1-800-765-6955.

Visit us at www.reviewandherald.com for information on other
Review and Herald® products.

FaceTime

BIBLE ANSWERS TO
TEENS' TOUGHEST
QUESTIONS

General Conference
of Seventh-day Adventists
Youth Ministries Department

REVIEW AND HERALD® PUBLISHING ASSOCIATION
Since 1861 | www.reviewandherald.com

Copyright © 2013 by the General Conference of Seventh-day Adventists Youth Ministries Department

12501 Old Columbia Pike
Silver Spring, Maryland 20904, USA

Published by Review and Herald® Publishing Association, Hagerstown, MD 21741-1119

All rights reserved. No portion of this book may be reproduced, stored in a retrieval system, or transmitted in any form or by any means (electronic, mechanical, photocopy, recording, scanning, or other), except for brief quotations in critical reviews or articles, without the prior written permission of the publisher.

Review and Herald® titles may be purchased in bulk for educational, business, fund-raising, or sales promotional use. For information, e-mail SpecialMarkets@reviewand herald.com

The Review and Herald® Publishing Association publishes biblically based materials for spiritual, physical, and mental growth and Christian discipleship.

Bible texts credited to NIV are from the *Holy Bible, New International Version*. Copyright © 1973, 1978, 1984, 2011 by Biblica, Inc. Used by permission. All rights reserved worldwide.

This book was
Edited by Paula Webber
Copyedited by Delma Miller
Designed by Daniel Anez / Review and Herald® Design Center
Cover art by © Thinkstock.com
Typeset: Minnion Pro 11/13

PRINTED IN U.S.A.

17   16   15   14   13   5   4   3   2   1

Library of Congress Cataloging-in-Publication Data
Face time : Bible answers to teens' toughest questions / General Conference Youth Ministries Department.
    p. cm.
1. Christian life—Textbooks. 2. Conduct of life—Textbooks. 3. Seventh-Day Adventists—Doctrines.
4. Christian teenagers—Religious life—Textbooks. 5. Christian teenagers—Conduct of life—Textbooks.
I. General Conference of Seventh-Day Adventists. Youth Ministries Dept.
  BX6155.F33 2012
  268′.4330882867—dc23

                    2012032770

ISBN 978-0-8280-2666-6

Acknowledgment

Special thanks to Kimberley Tagert-Paul,
an internationally published author whose passion for young
people shines from every page of this book.

Dear Reader,

It is with fervent prayer and great anticipation that we release *Face Time.* We hope that the biblical wisdom and insights you find here will draw you closer to Christ and challenge you to take a stand on some of the complex issues we face today.

Here is a navigation guide to the sections you'll find in each lesson:

Icebreaker: This is an introductory question, explanation, or short story that draws a practical connection between the subject of the lesson and the life of the youth.

Dig In: This section aims to connect the lesson to your emotions and experiences.

Hot Potato: This section includes perspectives on both sides of the issue; the lessons are aimed at helping you take a stand, and also prepare you for questions that may be asked.

Hot Potato Questions: These act as a follow-up to the hot potato section to facilitate further discussion and study.

Bible Discovery: A series of scriptures to ground each lesson and help you grow in faith.

Extra Gem: Supplemental quotations from the Spirit of Prophecy.

Sharing Time: This represents creative and practical ideas for sharing what you have learned through the study.

Consider This: A challenge for the week to apply the lesson to your daily life.

May God continue to bless you as you begin this journey with Him.

—General Conference of Seventh-day Adventist Youth Ministries Department

Contents

Abortion

a Christian perspective

This is a sensitive study, and opinions will vary about this issue. Be especially careful not to pass judgment while doing this study with your group. They may be affected by this topic on different levels. Maintain an atmosphere that will allow all individuals to be heard. You may never know the impact you will leave with them—or how it may help your young people with future decisions.

Icebreaker

No matter how you look at it, war is not pretty. What started in heaven with its catastrophic consequences spilled onto our planet, and person against person has followed in the course of history. The Bible describes battles of complete annihilation. Genocide is also part of biblical history.

Throughout time war has been a part of humanity's planning. As technology has advanced, the weapons of war have become more and more sophisticated, changing the landscape of wars. We know that war will continue on this earth as one person battles another—until a great final conflict will end war forever.

While war reshapes landmasses and countries, it also brings with it one of its greatest consequences—the loss of life.

In the twentieth century alone there have been more than 100 acts of war and genocide on our planet. And the cost in human life has been staggering—more than 160 million men and women perished. To put that number in perspective, that's approximately half of the current U.S. population, and those are just the known casualties from the 1900s.

Dig In

There is another battle going on for life. And the statistics for this battle are even more staggering. Regarding the amount of lives lost, it far exceeds the number of lives lost in worldwide conflicts from just this past century. What is this battle that is costing so many innocent lives? Abortion.

Abortion is a deliberate termination of pregnancy. It can be done at any point in the life of the fetus inside the womb. It almost always results in the death of the fetus. There have been several noted cases of a baby surviving attempted abortions, but those are rare.

Statistics are just that—statistics. Many things can affect the numbers. And in the case of abortion, that is even more true. Many abortions throughout the world go unreported. But of those that are, the numbers are staggering. Every day there are approximately 115,000 known abortions performed on our planet. That adds up to 42 million lives lost each year. Multiply that by the years in the century, and you'll see that millions more lives are lost to abortion than to war.

Hot Potato

Most of the nations of the world allow abortion for various reasons. Almost all of the world allows abortions to be performed if the life of the mother is in danger. Only Chile, El Salvador, Malta, Nicaragua, and the Vatican City outlaw abortion completely. (Leaders—see the following Web site for further information: www.pregnantpause.org/lex/world02map.htm.)

The issue of abortion has become about a woman's right to choose to end the life of her fetus. But does that right come at a cost?

What are women choosing to end through abortion? The heartbeat begins on the twenty-first day after conception—a time when most women are not even aware that they are pregnant. At 10 weeks the human body is completely formed. Fingerprints are already in place. The fetus' cells have already begun specializing—the outer layer of the fertilized egg becoming the nervous system, skin, and hair. The middle layer becomes the skeleton, muscles, circulatory system, kidneys, and sex organs. And the inner layer will become the breathing and digestive organs.

Many women who choose to end the life of their fetus do so at a high cost. Guilt and depression often accompany abortion. One woman who underwent abortions two times by her twenty-third birthday also tried to commit suicide three times by her twenty-seventh birthday as a result of her choices. That response isn't out of the ordinary. One young girl said that it hurts to see baby things because it brings back sad memories. Another stated that she thinks about it every day. She regrets her decision. She cautions others to think about whether the pain of nine months outweighs the pain of a lifetime.

So why do so many women choose abortion if it causes such pain? Eighty-three percent of abortions worldwide are performed in developing countries. Only 17 percent of abortions that are performed are done in developed countries. Most (75 percent) of those choosing abortion say that a baby would interfere with work, school, or other responsibilities. Those same individuals cite lack of finances as the main reason for not wanting a child at the time of the abortion. The largest majority of those choosing abortion belong to the lowest income levels. The cost of raising a child is high—especially in countries with weaker economies where the struggle to survive is extremely difficult.

Hot Potato Questions

- Who is the Creator of life? Does God care about every life that He creates?
- When do you think life begins? At conception? When a baby can live outside of the mother's womb?
- Why is it important to define when life begins? Can that make a difference in how you decide to view a fetus?
- If you had to make an important decision such as whether or not to have an abortion, where would you turn for guidance and help?
- Do you think that it is a woman's right to choose an abortion in cases of rape, or if the mother's life is in danger? Why or why not?
- Do you think God forgives us if we make a decision that goes against His will? Explain your answer.
- Is it easier to let God forgive us than to forgive ourselves?
- In studying about issues such as abortion, does it make more sense to follow God's original plan for sexual intimacy to be a part of marriage?

Bible Discovery

Psalm 139:13, 14. Why did King David say that he was "fearfully and wonderfully made"? What does that mean to you? As you study how the body works together to sustain life, do you think you are a miracle? Does God know us before we are born? Should that make a difference when we make a decision about abortion? Why or why not?

Psalm 22:9, 10. When does God consider us His creation? As the cells divide and create a body, does God already love and cherish the fetus? Babies are vulnerable and must depend on their mothers. Do you think that God wants us to have that same relationship with Him? Does that mean He can be trusted to help us, even in the hardest of times?

James 1:27. Whom does the Bible say we are to give care to? Can you see the principle that God wants us to care for those who are unable to care for themselves? Would that include unborn children? Why or why not? How can we help those that are not yet born? What kind of activities do you think a Christian should be involved with in relation to the fight for the unborn?

Psalm 51. This was written after David committed adultery with Bathsheba. As a result, they lost the child that was conceived because of that sin. Do you think David found the forgiveness he was seeking? Does God want to forgive us when we make mistakes? Verse 17 tells us that God wants only a contrite heart. Do you think someone who has chosen abortion can find peace in God? Why or why not?

1 John 1:9, 10 and **1 John 2:1, 2.** Do these verses promise that God will forgive our mistakes if we ask? In addition to forgiving, what else does He do? Does cleansing mean that our sins are washed away? When you wash the dirt out of your clothing, is it gone forever? God wants to do that for us, too. What does an advocate do? Is it good news to know that you have an advocate who talks to your heavenly Father about you? Can you trust Him to guide you in making the right choices for your life? Can you accept His forgiveness and can you offer it to others who may have made difficult choices?

EXTRA GEM

Ellen White wrote about the importance God places on our lives. Read what she wrote:

"Every one should consider the solemn question, What is my life toward God and my fellow-men? No man liveth unto himself. No life is simply neutral in its results. The enemy often blinds the mind in regard to the importance of life; but it is of vast importance, and we cannot cast off our responsibilities without imperiling our eternal interests. We shall be held accountable for doing our duty to God and to our fellow-men. Our false theories of life will not lessen the claims that are upon us, or make void the relation that exists between us and humanity. We cannot break the thread of our obligation to others. Our obligations not only concern this life, but are as far reaching as eternity, and we cannot fulfill them without divine aid. Our life was given us of God, and is dependent upon Him, as the leaf is dependent upon the bough for sustenance. What is Christian life? It is a life rescued, a life taken out of a world of sin, and attached to the life of Christ. It is the life of one to whom has been imputed the righteousness of Christ" (*Youth's Instructor*, June 21, 1894).

Sharing Time

Your friends may look to you for help in making difficult choices. What advice would you give them if they came to you when trying to make an important decision? Make a list of Bible verses you could use to help them choose the best for their life. Thinking about it ahead of time will help you be ready when they need you.

Consider This

Often the most difficult thing to do is to forgive ourselves. Have you made a decision that you regret? Know that God will forgive you—all you have to do is ask! Place whatever burden you are carrying into God's hands; then let Him carry that burden for you. Pray and ask God to do this; He will carry the load. Whenever the devil tempts you to pick the burden back up, tell him, "NO!" God will take it from you—all you have to do is ask and leave it with Him.

Abuse

when home sweet home isn't so sweet

This lesson can be an especially sensitive one. Often abuse is hidden well, especially within the church family. Cover this lesson with prayer and understanding, for you may be working with young people experiencing abuse themselves. Also, remind your young people that they should never put themselves in danger when trying to help someone in an abusive situation. Tell them to always go to someone to help them if they suspect abuse is taking place.

Icebreaker

More than 100 years ago a song was written that still brings a sense of wistfulness to its listeners. You won't hear it on the radio, but you may still hear it being sung around campfires. The words may not be familiar to you, but they were to American soldiers during the Civil War.

"'Mid pleasures and palaces though we may roam,
  Be it ever so humble, there's no place like home!"

Those are two lines from a song by John Howard Payne, which he later incorporated into an opera.

Close your eyes and imagine it's twilight, and the only sounds you hear are musical. No guns, no moaning of injured soldiers, no shouts of readiness, just the sounds of two bands playing: one on each side of their opposing camps brought together by their longing for home, singing the same song that, for the moment, unites them. This was the scene of many battlefields during the American Civil War. One band of musicians would start the song, and soon soldiers would begin singing. Soon the music would start on the enemy side, with soldiers ceasing their activities to join in. For a moment they weren't soldiers fighting against each other, but travelers longing for home.

For the author of "Home, Sweet Home," life ended far from his own home. He died and was buried in Tunis in 1852. It wasn't until 1883 that people, remembering Payne and his gift of song, brought his remains home to America. As his casket was brought onto land, a 65-piece band played his favorite and well-loved song. After thousands paid their respects to him in New York City, President Chester Arthur accompanied his body to Washington, D.C.'s famous Oak Hill Cemetery, where he was buried.

Dig In

John Payne's body may have been returned to his native country, but his home life had not been so sweet. He had struggled for many years and was a terrible money manager.

For many Christian families, home isn't so sweet either. Sadly, religion is not a deterrent when it comes to abuse. Statistics show that there is almost as much abuse going on in Christian homes as there is in homes without religion. In fact, it is estimated that one in three young people will experience some form of abuse in their homes.

It is also estimated that up to 56 percent of marriages fall victim to some form of abusive behavior. This is a sad reality for many.

Hot Potato

Abuse comes in many forms, but is almost always centered on power and control.

Abuse can be emotional, economic, sexual, physical, and even spiritual. Abusers use such tactics as isolation, mind games, withholding money, intimidation, manipulation of children and pets, control over decisions, and threats to gain power in a relationship. Abusers believe they have the right to hold supreme control over their partner or children. Abuse doesn't have boundaries, either—not gender, age, race, marital status, and sadly, not religious orientation. And for Christians, unfortunately, abuse at home is rarely reported.

Hot Potato Questions

- Why do you think God allows abuse, especially when children and women are involved? Do you think that it hurts Him too?
- How do we know that God has a tender heart for those who are most vulnerable?
- What do you think causes people to become abusive? Do you think abusers are victims themselves?
- Is there a line between discipline and abuse with children? Who draws that line? Why do you think this way?

- Is neglect a form of abuse? Why or why not?
- Do you think a person suffering from abuse should have to stay with their abuser? What if it is a young person?
- If there were someone in your church that you knew was suffering from abuse, where would you send them for help? Should abuse ever be kept quiet? Why or why not?
- Can the pain and shame of abuse be forgiven, and can healing take place?

Bible Discovery

Proverbs 13:24. Is this verse difficult to understand? Do you think that this verse means that a parent should use corporal punishment to discipline their children? What occupation mentioned in the Bible used a rod? Shepherds used rods. Did shepherds use rods to strike their sheep? The answer is no! The rod wasn't used to strike the sheep at all—it was used for guiding them. Does that help to make this verse clearer? God disciplines us, and sometimes it hurts. But that discipline brings us back in line with His will. Do you think that that is what Solomon was describing here? (See also Proverbs 23:13 and Proverbs 29:15.)

Galatians 5:19-25. Do you think that some of the characteristics in verses 19-21 are found in abusers? Can those characteristics be hidden? Why or why not? Could there be someone being abused in your church without you knowing about it? Do you think that God can change the heart of an abuser and replace the bad with the fruit of the Spirit? Should a person who has been abused be forced to forgive their abuser? Why do you think this way? Can you have the true Spirit and hold on to anger and hurt? Why or why not?

Matthew 18:6. Does Jesus have a special place in His heart for children? Why do you think He says that it will be so hard in judgment for those who hurt and abuse children? If Jesus cares so much for the helpless, shouldn't we also care for them? Is there anything we can do to help those who are being abused? Is it ever wrong to intervene? Can it be dangerous? Can you think of helpful ways to handle abusive situations?

Ephesians 6:1-4. What is the promise that this commandment gives to young people? Are obeying and honoring always the same thing? Do you think God requires you to obey someone who is telling you to do something against Him? Explain why you feel this way. What could you do if someone were causing you to break God's commandments? Do you have someone you could talk to about abuse if you needed to? Why might it be hard to talk about abuse with others? Do these verses tell us that there is to be a reciprocal relationship between a young person and their parents, both showing the character of their heavenly Father?

Isaiah 60:18. This verse is a promise. Where do you think this promise will take place? Does that mean we shouldn't work to end violence here and now? Abuse started because of sin. Will it end with sin? What can we do to encourage others to respect their partners and children? Can the hope of heaven help those who are suffering some form of abuse? What can you do to help make others aware of abuse, especially as it occurs within the walls of a Christian home?

EXTRA GEM

Ellen White was shown how true, godly love can transform our world. Read what she wrote: "Love's agencies have wonderful power, for they are divine. The soft answer that 'turneth away wrath,' the love that 'suffereth long, and is kind,' the charity that 'covereth a multitude of sins'—would we learn the lesson, with what power for healing would our lives be gifted! How life would be transformed and the earth become a very likeness and foretaste of heaven!" (*The Adventist Home,* p. 195).

Sharing Time
Learn the signs of a possible abuser. Don't be afraid to speak up if you feel someone needs your help.

Possible Warning Signs of an Abuser
- Controls all aspects of the victim's life
- Blames other people (including the victim) for their own problems and mistakes
- Shows cruelty toward animals and vulnerable people
- Excuses violent behavior after the fact
- Can suddenly be very moody and jealous
- Deprives victim of necessities
- Isolates victim from supportive friends and family

Consider This

Statistics say that one in three young people will experience some form of abuse in their lifetime. Maybe you never will, but chances are you will likely know someone who will. Be prepared. Whom would you turn to for help? What help would you be able to give? How do you feel about helping? Explore these thoughts and come up with a list of people, places, and ideas to offer others who might need your help. Remember, they may be vulnerable, but you can make a difference.

Blended Families

the Christian blended family

Remember that not all of your young people will come from traditional families. Blended families are more often the norm in our society. Helping your young people see the importance of their relationships and listening to them will help them in ways that can change their family dynamics for the better. Pray for all your families.

Icebreaker

Her name in French is Cendrillion, in German it is Aschenputtel, in Spanish it is Cenicienta, and in Afrikaans it is Asepoestertjie. The story of Cinderella is known all over the world. The fictitious story has Cinderella living in unfortunate circumstances with a dream for her life to change. And change does happen quickly! With the aid of her fairy godmother, Cinderella is transported and transposed. Her Prince Charming rescues her from her dreary world, and they live happily ever after—or so the story goes.

The tale probably originated around the first century B.C. In one version, Rhodopis (meaning rosy-cheeked) washes clothes in the Ormoc stream. Her Prince Charming is the pharaoh Amasis, who falls in love and marries her, taking her away from her dreary world.

Dig In

Whatever you call her, Cinderella has come to represent the changing state of marriage in our societies. When you mention the word "stepfamily," Cinderella's plight often comes to mind. No matter how hard she tried, Cinderella could not meet the approval of her stepmother or stepsisters. She was the one who did most of the housework in keeping their home neat and the food prepared. As a result, she almost missed her opportunity to live the life she dreamed of.

The opposite of the Cinderella story was the 1970s sitcom *The Brady Bunch*. In this fictional TV series, two single parents with three children each made the perfect blended family, along with a housekeeper and the family dog. Sure, they had their problems, but they worked them out, and the happy family smiled on.

So is either fictional family a true picture of what a blended family looks like? The answer is no. Each blended family (a family that combines one original parent with a new stepparent, along with children from previous marriages, and perhaps new children from the new marriage) is unique! No two are the same, nor do they function the same.

A blended family is much like an adoption. A decision has been made by some of the family to adopt new members into the family. In the case of a blended family, this is usually the decision of the partners in the new marriage. The children may agree to this new situation or they may not, but too often they are not given any choice in the matter. Battle lines may be drawn, and separate camps are formed.

Does it have to be this way? The answer is no. Stepfamilies involve people with more complex relationships, but they don't have to include battlegrounds. Just like any other family, the secret is to keep the whole relationship Christ-centered. If the family allows God to be their guide through the journey, it can and will be a successful blend of parents and children who love and respect each other.

Hot Potato

Unlike other marriage and family relationships, a blended family doesn't get the chance for a honeymoon period. These families hit the ground running. And there really isn't a way to prepare for the dynamics that will hit them. The mixture comes together quickly, and the feelings of some members may not be easily understood.

The children of the new parents may have conflicting feelings about the new blended family. Most want the one thing they may not get right away—security and stability, and they often have feelings that they can't completely define, but are definitely feeling.

Hot Potato Questions

- Are you part of a blended family? How did you feel when you knew that a new family unit was forming?
- Did you experience feelings of grief, anger, confusion, or sadness? How did you handle these feelings?
- Is it easier for you to take your anger out against your new parent in order to preserve your relationship with your natural parent? What do you think God thinks about this?

- Is there anything you can do differently that might help your family get along better?
- Do you feel loyalty toward your real parents affects how you feel about your new stepparent and stepbrothers/sisters?
- Can you accept that there may be conflicts in any family? Have you tried to find compromises within your new relationship?
- Do you spend quality time with each parent so that you can develop all of your relationships? Do you think that God loves blended families any different than families with original parents? Why or why not?

Bible Discovery

Matthew 12:25. Jesus was talking to the Pharisees when He said this. They accused Him of receiving His power from the devil. Can we apply the wisdom here to families? Can a family that is divided survive for very long? Why or why not? What dynamics in a blended family could cause potential conflict? What are some ways to help a blended family have a better relationship? (Leaders, you might want to mention such things as practicing kindness, patience, and respect. These are things that all families should be practicing. But they are especially important given the dynamics of a blended family.)

Ephesians 4:29-32. In a blended family, could speaking badly about others who aren't a part of the new family cause trouble? (Such as the original parent, other brothers or sisters, etc.) How could this affect relationships within the new family? In our church families, does doing this also cause trouble? In what ways, especially in a blended family, is it important to have respect for others? Why? How can we practice such things as kindness, compassion, and forgiveness in our families? Were we given an example of this in Christ's life and death?

1 Corinthians 13:13. Paul writes that love is the greatest quality. Can it be more difficult to love in a blended family? Why do you think this way? Can loving a new stepparent make you feel less loyal to your real parents? Are there different degrees of love in a blended family? How might these be different than in an original family? We are adopted into God's family. Does He love us differently because of it? How can we apply His love into new relationships?

Ephesians 6:1-4. The Bible tells us to obey our parents. This is the first commandment with a promise. Does the Bible say that this will always be an easy thing to do, especially within the dynamics of a blended family? Can such qualities as love, forgiveness, compassion, patience, and compromise make this easier? What could you do if you disagree with your parents? What could you do if you disagree with a stepparent? Would the way you handle a problem be different depending on whether you were dealing with your real parent or your stepparent? Should you still honor and respect each of them? Why or why not? Why do you think the Bible verse tells fathers not to exasperate their children? What could this do to help children respect their parents?

Matthew 26:38. What does this verse tell us about Jesus' understanding of a support system? If Jesus felt the need for support, should we feel any different? Where can you find the support you need within your family? Within the church? Is there good support and bad support? Why do you feel this way? What kinds of qualities should you look for when trying to find the support you need?

EXTRA GEM

Ellen White was shown the importance of the family relationship. Read what she wrote: "The restoration and uplifting of humanity begins in the home. The work of parents underlies every other. Society is composed of families, and is what the heads of families make it. Out of the heart are 'the issues of life' (Proverbs 4:23); and the heart of the community, of the church, and of the nation is the household. The well-being of society, the success of the church, the prosperity of the nation, depend upon home influences" (*The Ministry of Healing,* p. 349).

Sharing Time

One of the most damaging things that happens in blended families is talking badly about the other natural parent. Do you know someone who is part of a blended family? You can help by helping them make a list of good qualities for all the parents involved. Write them down and review the list with your friend. Help them see that their new stepparent has good qualities too, and can be a positive part of their life. Show them how focusing on the positive can help to change the negative. You'll be a treasured friend for helping them see with new eyes!

Consider This

Make a list of the important qualities that you think a family should have. How many of these do you find in your family? Are some of them missing? If so, look at the list and see if there is one thing that you can focus on and try to help your family obtain. Pray about it and ask your heavenly Father how you can help your family find this missing quality. Be patient. It will be worth it in the end!

Bullying

emotional, verbal, and physical abuse

This is an ever-increasing issue facing more and more youth. You may not even be aware that bullying is an issue among your group, but this is a critical issue with young people today. Do your research and seek to help your young people.

Icebreaker

Ever hear the term *flying under the radar?* It has a historical meaning that doesn't date back that far. In the 1950s the military came up with the term for aircraft that would fly beneath radio detection and ranging. It was a way to escape detection by enemy forces.

Today the term is used around the world and is common in pop culture. It can be used in many ways—as a compliment, an insult, or advice. With the explosion of reality TV shows, it has also become an important strategy. Flying under the radar can actually get you pretty far in some situations. It's a way of doing things without making enemies, and it can keep you in the game until a time when you can gain control and get closer to the prize.

In life most people prefer to remain "under the radar." There are far more followers than leaders in the world. People don't like to call attention to themselves. It means less scrutiny. It means they can do their own thing without others interfering. It means they have more control over their own world. And that's not all bad, is it?

But there is an emerging group of individuals that are flying "under the radar." They have an ultimate goal, and chances are you have been a victim of their scheming at one time or another.

Dig In

Who are these people and how have they affected you? They are known as bullies. Bullies are aggressive people who intimidate or mistreat weaker people. And they are usually very good at what they do. They thrive on control and power, and what they do is most often premeditated and intentional.

In times past, bullying was usually done in the schoolyard, and it involved physical torment. But today's bullies are much smarter. They are now more secretive, and instead of using their fists, they use electronics.

Cyberbullying is the newest way to bully. The bully has now gone digital. It is estimated that 34 percent of all young people have experienced some sort of cyberbullying. Electronic aggression has replaced physical aggression as cyberbullies use text messaging, cell phones, and computers to spread online rumors on social networking sites. Their tactics include humiliation, destructive messages, gossip, and slander to inflict harm on their fellow peers. The fact that the size of the audience increases with technological bullying makes the humiliation even greater. Technology makes it a continuing form of aggression that can be done 24-7.

The problem is that most bullies don't even think of themselves as bullies. They don't understand that what they are doing is wrong, and they don't admit to doing it. They enjoy the feeling of power it gives them—an endorphin rush. Most bullies lack empathy, and they don't feel the pain of their victims.

Hot Potato

Have you ever wanted to get more attention? Do you like to get what you want? Would you like to gain more respect from people? Would you like to be more popular? How would you like to feel better about yourself? Would you like to do something you think is fun and punish others, especially those you are jealous of?

One way to do that is to be a bully, because those are the reasons most bullies give for their actions.

Childhood bullies are more likely to commit a crime by the time they are in their mid-20s, and they will probably become more violent as they age. They have a tendency to use drugs, alcohol, and tobacco products. They might be more likely to get into fights and probably be more likely to steal things and think there's nothing wrong with it. Still think it is OK?

What is bullying? It includes such things as leaving others out of a group activity. It can mean giving someone the "silent treatment." Most certainly it means using others to get what you want—using them only for your gain. It means making fun of others who are different, whether you do it in person by physical or verbal means, making faces or gestures that hurt, or using electronic media to damage feelings. It includes name-calling, teasing, gossiping, and spreading rumors. It also includes embarrassing others to humiliate them.

So does the Bible have anything to say about bullies? Plenty.

Hot Potato Questions
- Have you ever bullied someone else? If yes, why do you feel you have the right to do it? If no, have you ever been bullied?
- Have you ever fought back? Do you think you have the right to fight back against a bully?

Bible Discovery
Matthew 23:1-7. Jesus dealt with bullies. In His day they had a name—Pharisee. They held power over the people, and they loved to abuse it. Jesus spoke out against them in these verses. What did He say was the motivation for their behavior? Did He encourage others to be like them? Does it surprise you that Jesus called out the bullies? How do you think you can apply this to your life today?

Luke 4:28-30. What did Jesus do when others (the bullies) tried to hurt Him? Did He fight back? Did He let them get their way? Do you think that walking away can be an option that would work in your life? Why or why not?

1 Corinthians 1:27-31. People portray power and control as attributes to be desired. Is that what the Bible says? Why do you think God chooses certain things to point out the problems of others? Can you think of other verses in the Bible that show how God loves and cares for the lowly and despised? What about the sparrows? (Leaders may need to encourage the youth to think of other verses.)

Mark 10:45. Did Jesus want to have power and control over people? What does the Bible say that Jesus came to do? Would a bully ever be a servant? Why or why not? Is it easy to follow Jesus' example when you are being bullied? How can you be a servant to others who try to have control over you?

Matthew 22:39. What would happen if we started to see others in the same way we see ourselves (as God sees us)—all on an equal plane? If we look at others differently than ourselves, could that lead to intolerance and bullying? From this verse, how does God want you to see others? Can we use this verse to help us end bullying?

EXTRA GEM

Ellen White faced trials, especially after being chosen as a servant of God. Listen to what she says about the trials we must face, and the way to face them:

"It is not a great work and great battles alone which try the soul and demand courage. Everyday life brings its perplexities, trials, and discouragements. It is the humble work which frequently draws upon the patience and the fortitude. Self-reliance and resolution will be necessary to meet and conquer all difficulties. Secure the Lord to stand with you, in every place to be your consolation and comfort" (*Testimonies for the Church*, vol. 3, p. 81).

Sharing Time

Do you know of someone who is being bullied? What can you do to help them? Make a list of at least five things you can do to help someone being bullied. Here are some ideas: Stand beside them! Get their permission to help them. Having a friend to help may give them the confidence they need to gain back the control they have lost. Help them seek adult help if they need it. Help them formulate a plan and a solution. Most of all, be a good role model for them! Choose not to be a bully.

Consider This

Do you use electronic media often? Have you seen others being bullied online? What have you done to stop it? This week, be aware of others and watch for signs of bullying—people who have few friends, people who feel sad or rejected, someone who might cry easily and avoids eye contact. Make a choice to be their friend and help them. If you make that choice, others may feel that they can do the same, and you just might start something big—an end to bullying!

Creation
creation, evolution, cloning

See the notes contained in the study. The purpose of this study isn't so much to convince as it is to show young people the wonderful character of God and let them fall in love with Him all over again.

Icebreaker

Have you ever looked at an old-fashioned quilt and been attracted to the colors and patterns painstakingly sewn together? Or have you ever marveled at how light comes through stained glass and transforms the colors and patterns? If so, then you love pattern and color, just as God does! Of course, that's an easy conclusion to come to, isn't it? We see patterns everywhere. But have you taken a closer look at some of them?

For instance, there appears to be a remarkable pattern in the hatching time of eggs. The eggs of a potato bug generally hatch in seven days; those of a canary, 14; barnyard hens, 21. Are you beginning to see a pattern? Geese and duck eggs usually take 28 days. Ostrich eggs hatch in 42 days. Can you see the pattern now? It's easy, isn't it? They are all multiples of seven—God's perfect seven. Read on . . .

God's wisdom is further revealed in arrangements of sections and segments. Watermelons have an even number of stripes on their rinds. Ears of corn have an even number of rows on their husks. Oranges have an even number of segments. Stalks of wheat have an even number of grains. And this list goes on and on.

It's also possible that God has left us clues in our foods that tell us what part of the body they are good for. A sliced carrot looks like the human eye. And yes, science shows us carrots are great for the eye—both for function and blood flow! Think about a tomato. It has four chambers and is red. Is there anything in your body that looks like that? Of course! Your heart. And guess what scientists now know? Tomatoes are loaded with lycopenes and are pure heart food! Think about a walnut. What does it look like? Your brain. Just look at the wrinkles and folds—the shell resembles both halves of the neocortex. And what have scientists discovered about the walnut? It helps more than three dozen neurotransmitters involved in the brain's function.

Dig In

Consider the avocado. It resembles the womb. Scientists have shown us that eating this green fruit will balance hormones, help shed weight, and prevent some cervical cancers.

God has planted Himself all around us so that all we have to do is stop and take the time to look; we won't be able to miss Him. That's not the same as the ever-popular theory of God in all nature and the worship of it. That's called pantheism. Rather we are talking about finding the Creator in the created—something far different. Without a Bible or someone to tell you, it would still be possible to know your heavenly Father by studying His second book—nature!

Hot Potato

Some people like to put on blinders. They look at the things that God created and claim that they came from microscopic matter—nonliving matter at that! Could we really have evolved from monkeys? Could visiting the nearest zoo on a sunny afternoon be considered a family reunion of sorts?

Charles Darwin thought so when he set off on a voyage with Captain Robert FitzRoy on the H.M.S. *Beagle*. Their mission was to chart the coastline of South America. Five years later Darwin returned with "evidence and celebrity" and furthered his theory in "natural selection."

His book, published in 1859, *On the Origin of Species*, became the scientific textbook on evolutionary biology.

For years now, scientists have been trying to tie up all the loose ends in Darwin's theory. Their latest claim adressing the "missing link" was announced at a huge press conference in May 2009: Ida—a remarkable fossil that resembles a lemur—was their proof. Within hours of the conference, claims were shot down within the scientific community. Ida was just a well-preserved fossil!

Hot Potato Questions
- So how do you think humans came to be on this earth? Did God create them, or did they evolve from inorganic matter?
- Do scientists have a case for "natural selection"? Why or why not?
- Scientists are able to take living cells and clone living things. Do you think that God likes what people are doing in this area? Why or why not?

- Won't cloning help cure diseases and provide cures for people in pain? Doesn't that make it a good thing?
- To get the DNA needed to clone new organs, embryos would have to be destroyed.

What do you think of this? When do you think life begins? When do evolutionists think life begins? When do you think God says life begins?

Bible Discovery

Genesis 1. If the Bible is true, who created everything that is on earth? Do you believe this account of Creation? Why or why not? Do you believe what the Bible says as truth?

Do you think that God created the world in six literal days? Would that make it the same cycle that we are using today for our week? What does it say about the character of God? If He is the same yesterday, today, and forever (see Hebrews 13:8), then doesn't that consistency speak of strength you can trust?

Genesis 1:26, 27. By whose authority does the Bible say humanity was created? Who helped in the creation of them? In whose image were they created? Does this dispel completely the theory of evolution? Why do you think this way? If God is the author of life, do people have the right to also create life, i.e., cloning? (See also John 1:1-3.)

Genesis 1:28-30. What responsibility did God give to humanity at Creation? If they were to protect and nurture life, how would cloning fit into that responsibility? Would cloning put them in God's position of authority? Why or why not? God seeks a personal relationship with each individual. How would evolution change that thought if evolution were true? How about cloning? Do you think people have the judgment required to govern cloning and the technology that would be created as a result? Would it be used only for good?

Psalm 139:13-16. When does King David say that God personally knew him? In these verses do we see that God not only knew David but already had a plan for his life? If God knew David before he was born, did God also know you and already have a plan for you before you were even born? Could David (or you) believe in this if the theory of evolution were true? Why or why not? Does knowing this tell you of a loving Creator? (See also Isaiah 49:1-5 and Luke 1:8-20.)

Deuteronomy 10:17-19. What do these verses tell us about how God values each individual? Are we here to protect and defend life, or to live as we want to? Does God tell us to especially protect the vulnerable? What common factor do the fatherless, the widows, and the foreigners have? (Leaders, help your young people see that the widows and orphans have a common factor: a missing person from the family unit—parent/spouse.) God established the first family in Eden and used it as the basic unit for relationships. Could cloning undermine the family relationship? Why do you think this way? Do you believe the Bible because some scientific proposals agree with it, or because the knowledge found in the Bible is God's Word?

EXTRA GEM

Ellen White lived during the period that evolution was being brought to the front of scientific study. Read what she wrote about the dangers of teaching it: "In the study of science, as generally pursued, there are dangers equally great. Evolution and its kindred errors are taught in schools of every grade, from the kindergarten to the college. Thus the study of science, which should impart a knowledge of God, is so mingled with the speculations and theories of men that it tends to infidelity" (*Education*, p. 227).

Sharing Time

Your friends may ask you, "Where is there proof of God?" How can you answer them? Prepare yourself to answer this question, which you might be asked sometime in your life. Can you point them to specific things in nature that could never have occurred if life evolved? What evidence from your life has helped you believe there is a God? Write your answer to this question down and add your thoughts to it periodically so that you will be able to defend your faith. (See 1 Peter 3:15.)

Consider This

Do some research on the patterns of God in nature this week. Find at least one other item that you can point to that shows God in His creation. (Leaders, do your research beforehand and help your youth find clear examples. Look at such things as an elephant (four legs that are fulcrums) or a slice of cauliflower (looks like the brain and contains choline, shown to help memory). Another pattern is that creation happened in the order it was needed to sustain life. Everything people needed was provided before their creation. It gets to be a lot of fun finding these and should make the study a fun one for your youth!

Dating

dating, relationships, hooking up

Leaders, some of your young people may not be of dating age yet. You may be surprised, however, to know that young people are "hooking up" at earlier ages than ever before. You have a chance to guide them to God's plans for their young lives. Lead them to begin praying for their future mate now, even though they don't know whom it will be. It will help them to make wiser choices—God's way.

Icebreaker

There's no doubt you played the game when you were younger. You might have even played it recently. It has many variations. Even adults sometimes get into the act. Musical chairs. You know, the one in which you line up in a circle around a set of chairs, only there is one less than the group. You march around until the music stops, then everyone scrambles for a seat, only for one person to come up empty-handed—or in this case—empty-seated. The game goes on until just two people and one chair are left. Then it's all-out mayhem trying to capture that one chair. But someone does, and the winner is announced.

It is a game played around the world and with many different variations. Most admit the original title was Going to Jerusalem, which is the name cited in the famous *Bobbsey Twins* books, but the game no doubt goes back further than that. It is still popular today, even at adult gatherings. One of the variations played is called musical bumps. This is played without chairs, with the last person seated on the ground eliminated. Another fun variation is extreme musical chairs. In this variation, before sitting down the players must complete a task that was given to all before the round started. The music stops, players complete the task (such as: do five jumping jacks, touch the wall, sing a silly rhyme), then dive for the nearest chair. The one left standing is eliminated, and the game goes on. Other variations include hopping, jumping, and walking backward around the chairs.

Although the game is essentially the same, the names change around the world. The Cantonese variation translates to Fighting for Chairs. In German it is called Journey to Jerusalem, while in Japan it is called The Game of Stolen Chairs. Romania has perhaps the most unusual variation, called Birdie, Move Your Nest. Perhaps the Swedish have the best idea, though. They call their game The Whole Sea Is Storming.

Whatever you call it, it is usually just plain fun.

Dig In

Young people sometimes play a game similar to musical chairs. In this game they often hop from one situation to another, just as in musical chairs. They call this game "dating," *only dating isn't a game and shouldn't be considered one by Christian young people.* Sure, dating is fun. But its purpose, according to God's Word, is very different from how the world perceives it.

Before you even consider dating, you need several things in your life. Maturity is the first. Age isn't always the litmus test for being ready to date—maturity is a better gauge. Another aspect of your life that involves being ready to date is a sense of responsibility. Not only will it affect your life—dating will also affect each person you go out with. That's a lot of responsibility, and you have to be ready to take that on. Emotional stability is another area affected when you date. But the most important aspect of your life is to have a relationship with God. A right relationship with Him will provide guidance that will make the whole experience what it was meant to be. And God has more in store for you than what you see around you.

Hot Potato

Most youth have a life plan—what you want to be when you grow up and how you are going to make that happen. Being focused helps to make goals happen.

As young people, though, there are so many distractions that can pull you away from your plan. Your focus will be challenged, and sometimes that is a good thing, and sometimes not.

Dating should never be your number one focus. Sure, everyone wants to date eventually. That's all part of God's plan. But making it the focus of your young life can lead to severe consequences. You have other goals that you don't want to lose sight of—things such as education and employment. These things will give you a foundation from which to build a future. The distractions of dating may keep you from achieving your goals and all that God has planned for you.

Hot Potato Questions

- What age do you think is a good age to start dating? Or do you think that it isn't about age at all? Why or why not? What do you think is the end purpose in dating?

- Is courtship different than dating? Do you think that Christians should have a different attitude toward dating than the world does?
- Ask yourself, "Why do I want to date?"
- Do you have an idea what God's plan is for your life? Would dating fit in with that plan now, or in the future?
- Can you have a good social life without one-on-one dating?

Bible Discovery

Genesis 2:22-24. Why did God create woman? Do you think that God intended for man and woman to be united for their entire lives? Is there one true person for each of us? Why or why not? Do you trust God to lead you to the person you are meant to be with when the time is right? What do you think is the beauty in finding the right person and being the right person?

Proverbs 4:23. Why do you think Solomon—the wisest king ever—told his son to "guard your heart"? Had Solomon followed his own advice? Do you think that might have been why he told his son to guard his heart above all other things? What is involved with guarding your heart? If you are dating a lot, can you guard your heart? Why or why not? Can you develop friendships with the opposite sex and not date? How will these relationships help you as you mature, and will they help you guard your heart? (Leaders, make sure you define courtship/dating versus friendship.)

1 Corinthians 13:4-7. Here is an excellent text explaining what true love is. Can you use this list as you are dating to find out what love is supposed to be? Is it a good measuring stick to hold your relationship against? If you use it point by point, will it help you know if your relationship is headed in the right direction? Are these qualities of love a good prayer list for a future mate?

Deuteronomy 7:3; 2 Corinthians 6:14. What does the Bible say about dating unbelievers? Is that always easy to follow as a young person? There is a new trend that is called "missionary dating." (Leaders, this is dating for the purpose of winning someone to Christ.) How do you feel about this type of dating? Does something you do with noble intentions always work out for the good? Do you know anyone who has dated with this in mind? Statistics show that this type of dating rarely works out. Why do you think that might be? What is the risk for the Christian dating an unbeliever? Could it easily lead to backsliding? How easy would it be to have your ethics and morals compromised while dating a nonbeliever?

Titus 2:11-14. How can you lead a godly life with everything so crazy around you? This verse tells us to say no to worldly passions. Does that include dating? Why or why not? Is recreational dating something that Christians should be involved with? (Leaders, this is dating for the sake of dating, not for finding a mate.) What gives you the strength to say no to the things God does not have in mind for you—is it your strength or God's grace? Will you make a choice to listen to what God says about dating?

EXTRA GEM

Ellen White cared a lot about young people, and the Lord gave her guidance to share with them. Read what she wrote about Jesus and marriage: "He who gave Eve to Adam as a helpmeet performed His first miracle at a marriage festival. In the festal hall where friends and kindred rejoiced together, Christ began His public ministry. Thus He sanctioned marriage, recognizing it as an institution that He Himself had established" (*Letters to Young Lovers*, p. 14).

Mrs. White also saw how youth would let their senses take control—both in her time and the time to come. Read what she writes here and notice what she says about grace: "The senses will be guarded. The soul that has Jesus abiding in it will develop into true greatness. The intelligent soul who has respect unto all of God's commandments, through the grace of Christ, will say to the passions of the heart as he points to God's great moral standard of righteousness, 'Hitherto shalt thou come, but no further: and here shall thy proud waves be stayed,' and the grace of Christ shall be as a wall of fire round about the soul" (*Medical Ministry,* p. 143).

Sharing Time

Sooner or later your friends will come to you for advice about dating. Make a list of things you think are important to share with them about when and why to date. Include questions they should ask themselves, and that you should ask yourself about how you can know when you are ready to date and whom you should be dating. Include in your list your dating rights and responsibilities as you see them. (Leaders, this is a good activity to do as a group also. Let the youth list their dating rights and responsibilities as they see them—and copy the list for each youth.)

Consider This

Make a list of the qualities you want in a mate. Look again at 1 Corinthians 13 and use it as a guide. Begin praying now for your future mate. Ask your parents to pray with you about this person. Praying now will help God lead you in the future, and help both of you be prepared for the happiness God has in mind for you. Praying for that person also helps you focus on your priorities and will help you when choosing when and whom you will date.

Death and Grieving

life, death, and the resurrection of Christ

Read about the stages of death before presenting this topic to your young people. Be very gentle, and listen as they speak on this subject. Youth are particularly vulnerable to death and dying and often fear even studying about it.

Icebreaker

His name is Richard Sandrak. Born in the Ukraine, he became famous as "Little Hercules," because he was known as the strongest boy in the world. By age 2 he was working out with his parents, who decided to train him as a prodigy. By age 6 his pictures stunned the world because of his lean, toned body and the eight-pack his stomach showed. Unfortunately, his fame didn't follow him as he grew up. It became known that his body, with only 1 percent body fat, wasn't without controversy. His father, Pavel, was feeding him a supplement that is reported to have contained steroids. What was cute at 12 hasn't followed him into young adulthood. Still, he hopes to someday have a career in the movie industry. Strong isn't always mighty!

Then there is Varya Akulova. Now 20, she was born in the Ukraine also. But her strength has come naturally. Her parents are both very strong, and Varya has picked up the family strength gene. Growing up in a poor family in a rural and isolated part of the Ukraine, she didn't gain her strength from steroids. She ate little if any meat, mostly because her family could not afford it. Though she doesn't have the look of a bodybuilder, her feats of strength are amazing. She has appeared twice in the *Guinness Book of World Records* as the strongest girl in the world. She can lift a 150-pound dumbbell off the ground with just one hand. With her legs she can lift 500 pounds without a problem. She defeats her 250-pound father at wrestling, even though she weighs only 85 pounds. She is a well-rounded athlete, participating in aerobatics, juggling, running, arm wrestling, kickboxing, and power lifting. Both her upper body and lower body are equally strong. At age 12 she lifted several people on her back while lifting two kettleballs off the ground at the same time—an astounding total weight of 775 pounds (352 kilograms).

Varya lives in relative obscurity, yet hopes someday to win an Olympic medal for her country. Her family would love to promote how health and fitness can keep young people from being overweight and prevent such diseases as diabetes and obesity. She is a great student and an accomplished painter. What drives her? Not her parents. They allow her to train only if she wants to. For Varya, being strong is fun, but it is not the only focus in her life.

Dig In

So are young people like Richard and Varya examples of true strength? Will their strength protect them from the trials that even young people have to sometimes experience? Unfortunately, no. There are things that naturally happen in life that their strength does not shield them from.

You, too, have a source of strength that can make you strong when bad things happen. Your heavenly Father is right beside you, ready to lend you His strength.

Perhaps you have needed that strength when you experienced the death of a family member or friend. If not, someday the inevitable will happen, and you will need to rely on Jesus to help heal a pain that can change your life. It's a part of life. And knowing about grief and mourning—talking about death and life—can help when the time comes.

Hot Potato

No one likes to talk about death. Why? While we celebrate life, we mourn at its loss. And it is hard to talk with those who experience death's tearing away of a loved one. Yet talking is one of the healthiest forms of healing for those experiencing loss.

Death is not something you can prepare for. The crushing pain of loss will be there no matter how many times you experience it. Losing a loved one will inevitably remind you of another loss, and the pain starts all over again. The only way to prevent this pain is to detach yourself from everyone; then you won't miss them if they are gone. But that makes no sense, does it? Loving is a risk, but one that is worth the cost.

As Christians, we have knowledge that death does not have to be the end of life. Choosing the Savior as your own and living a life for Him means that a resurrection day will come—and with it, no more death! The comfort God gives us in this promise helps at a time when we simply cannot rely on our own strength.

Those grieving are often told to "be strong." But as young people, you are already dealing with so much change in your life, that facing another change can be overwhelming. Then we might forget the Father's strength and become overwhelmed at the loss of someone we love. Especially for young people, this becomes an issue. Then such things as depression, sleep problems, academic troubles, risky behaviors, and denial can make the healing process more difficult. If you or a friend experiences these symptoms after a loss, you must talk with an adult who can help you. Parents, teachers, and counselors are all available to help. Safe and nurturing outlets are needed during this difficult time.

Hot Potato Questions
- Why do you think death is especially hard for young people to handle?
- Is it harder to lose someone older or a friend your age? Why do you think that way?
- As a Christian, do you think you should grieve differently than others? Why or why not?
- Have you lost someone close to you? If so, what things helped you to heal? In what ways do you think you can reach out to others and help as they experience loss?
- What can you do to help preserve someone's memory?

Bible Discovery
Romans 6:23. This is a promise! Sin brings death, but because of Jesus' death, believers have the promise of eternal life. What does the Bible mean that the "wages of sin is death"? What are the wages of following Christ? Can this promise be a comfort to those who are grieving?

Romans 8:38. What does Paul say can separate us from the love of God? Can death separate us from God? If the person is sleeping in the grave—which is what the Bible calls death—what promise do they have that they will see God and their loved ones again? If you are grieving, will God understand, even though He knows you will see the person again? Does God help those who are mourning?

1 Peter 1:3, 4. How can we have a "living hope" (NIV)? Can anything take that hope away from us? Can we choose to give up that hope? When you are in the middle of grieving, is it hard to always remember that living hope? Do you think God understands this? Why or why not? Does having this hope help in the grieving process?

John 11:14-43. This is the story of Lazarus and his resurrection from the dead. What did Jesus Himself call death? Do you think that if Lazarus had already been in heaven that Jesus would have called him back to this earth? Why or why not? Did Jesus care that His friends were hurting? What did He do in verse 35? If Jesus wept over a loved one, do you think He understands when we do? Twice it mentions that Jesus was deeply moved. Does that tell you He understands your losses too? What did Jesus call Himself in verses 25, 26? Ask yourself the same question Jesus asked Martha: Do you believe this? Jesus said that He asked all this of the Father so that others may believe. Can this hope be something you can share with others to help them at a time of personal loss?

2 Samuel 12:16-24. (Leaders, read the whole chapter to get a better perspective of what was going on and what caused David's grief and repentance.) Was David grieving? Did you know that physiologists say that the death of a child is the most difficult death to deal with? Was David afraid to mourn in front of others even though he was the king? Did David understand that death is a sleep? Did he expect someday to be reunited with his son? After David went through his mourning, what did he do next? Can this be an example for us, that after grief life will go on? Did acting this way diminish David's grief? Should we be careful not to diminish others' grief but support them and offer them hope?

EXTRA GEM

Ellen White experienced grief and understood that God comforts us to enable us to comfort others. Read what she wrote and take courage from it: "It is your privilege to receive grace from Christ that will enable you to comfort others with the same comfort wherewith you yourselves are comforted of God. . . . Let each try to help the next one. Thus you may have a little heaven here below, and angels of God will work through you to make right impressions. . . . Seek to help wherever you can. Cultivate the best dispositions that the grace of God may rest richly upon you" (*God's Amazing Grace*, p. 122).

Sharing Time
There are five stages of grief that are part of the normal process. Not everyone grieves the same, so don't expect your friends to grieve as you do. Learn more about the stages: denial, anger, bargaining, depression, and acceptance. Then, when you or a friend experiences loss, you will understand that many of the things felt are normal. If they go on for extended periods of time or cause other symptoms, you will be ready to reach out and find the help you or another needs. Be ready to listen. Listening is the best help next to sharing God's comfort with them.

Consider This
Look up the story behind the hymn "It Is Well With My Soul."

A good place is the following link: www.hymns.net/stories/spafford. htm. Not only are the words a real inspiration at the time of loss, but the story behind the hymn is even more inspiring. When you or another experiences loss, remember this brave man and the words that he wrote from a grieving heart. Look at the assurance he had and know that you can have it too!

Decisions
how to design your future

This is a self-contained study. It would be good for individuals or in a group setting. It would be good to review Judges 6:36-40 and *Patriarchs and Prophets,* chapter 53, to see how Gideon used a fleece to interpret God's will.

Icebreaker

You are about to enter uncharted territory. You are all alone. Everything about your mission depends on the decisions you are about to make. Are you ready?

You see trees before you. Lots of trees. So what will you take to survive through the forest that is before you? Food and water—no one would forget those. So what else do you need? A sleeping bag in case you get trapped and it gets cold; a large knife for cutting tough vines; and extra socks in case yours get wet. Your list is getting longer. Have you forgotten anything?

Oh, yeah! You finally remember. You need a compass.

A compass is a tool that helps someone navigate. A magnetic compass always points to true north. There are now more modern ways of determining direction that don't depend on the magnetic poles of our earth, but the good old-fashioned compass is still a valuable tool.

Before the invention of the compass, sea travel was especially difficult. Most mariners stayed close to shore. They had to depend on things such as landmarks and the night sky to navigate their way around. The compass allowed man to move about and explore. So what happened if it was a foggy night?

Teens are doing just that: moving about and exploring their world. But like ancient mariners, you too need a compass to help you navigate through your future.

Do you have one? If you have your Bible handy, then yes you do! The Bible is God's compass—a gift to us to help us make the decisions that we are called on to make.

Dig In

Adam and Eve were the first humans to have to make decisions. One of Adam's first decisions was to name the animals that God created. Can you imagine that scene . . .

"His name?" Adam laughed, and the corners of his eyes wrinkled with pleasure.

He watched the creature dance among the clover, leaping and bounding with life.

"His name shall be Lamb. He will be my favorite. I'll keep him close to my heart, for he lives his joy, the joy I feel here"—Adam spread his arms wide—"in the garden with You."

God laughed and smiled His delight at His newborn son. He looked into his face, the image of His Father. What joy Adam brought to His Father's heart.

What a time God and Adam must have had together that day. Adam making wise decisions and sharing them with his Father. Too bad that later he would make a decision that would change the world forever. Good decisions and bad decisions. How do you know what to choose and how to plan as you navigate through these rough teen years and into the future God planned for you?

Hot Potato

"We've already come this far." Ever heard those words? Perhaps on a drive with your parents, perhaps when deciding on dating. Many people feel that they've already invested too much time, money, or emotions to turn back, even though it is clear they are heading in the wrong direction. Ever feel that way? Don't be afraid to turn back. TURN BACK!

Continuing to go in the wrong direction isn't going to get you any closer to the goal.

"Everyone else seems to think this is right." Ever heard those words? You've probably used them yourself. Just because everyone else says it is right doesn't make it so. It's a good way to be led way off track. Look at those who died at the Waco complex of the Branch Davidians. Everyone assumed that their leader, David Koresh, was right. Seventy-six people died on that fateful day in April 1993, including 17 children. Sometimes others may be right, but you need to use wisdom before making decisions based on someone else's knowledge.

"Oh, that, that's easy!" It's called overconfidence, and it leads to many mistakes. Yes, it's good to have confidence in your abilities. Confidence usually means that you have studied, practiced, and learned that you can do what you are setting out to do. Confidence comes from hard work. But overconfidence can lead to careless mistakes and bad decisions. Don't get caught up in this trap. You are too smart for that, right?

How do you make the best decisions for you?

Hot Potato Questions

- Have you ever made a bad decision? What were the consequences of that decision?
- Did you need help in correcting the problems caused by your decision? How do you think God feels when we make poor decisions?
- Do you think using the fleece method is a good way to make decisions? Explain your answer.
- Have you ever tried a "fleece" answer? Why or why not.

Bible Discovery

Jeremiah 29:11. Do you believe that God has a plan for your life? Do you believe that He created you with a purpose in mind? Do you sometimes feel that you have gone outside of that plan? Can you get back on track with God? God says in this verse that He not only has a plan for your life, but He also wants to give you a future and a hope. Maybe the first step in making decisions is to come to God and believe.

Jeremiah 33:3. Who is going to answer your questions and help make decisions for you? Does God promise that He will do this with you? Do you believe enough to allow God to show you the things you need to know? Let God prove to you that He will do this for you by trusting Him in all areas of your life. God can be trusted. You need to learn that for yourself.

Joshua 1:8. God's Word is the compass we need to help us navigate our way through life. How can you meditate on it day and night? What do you think this means? In what ways can you carry God's Word into your decision-making? Do you trust the principles in God's Word to lead you onto the right paths? How can you grow to believe that even more? Does meditating on God's Word include things such as prayer?

Mark 11:24; Isaiah 26:3. How can things such as prayer and finding God's peace help us make decisions for our lives? Do you believe that God will answer your prayers when you pray for wisdom? Does having a deep sense of peace about a decision help you feel that God is blessing that decision? Are there times that we cannot trust our emotions? Is having a sense of peace different from emotional feelings?

Matthew 25:23. In what ways can you grow in your decision-making with God? Is it better to start with small steps and grow from there or to take big leaps? Why do you feel this way? The faithful servant had used wise strategy that was developed over time. How can you develop your strategies to succeed in life as the servant did? Is being faithful in the small stuff a step in the right direction to lead you to bigger and better things? The wise servant knew that he shouldn't quit when it came to the master's business. Is quitting a good strategy for your life? If you quit, will you leave the victory to someone else?

EXTRA GEM

Ellen White understood how hard it was as a young person to make right choices and good decisions.

"We should be pervaded with a deep, abiding sense of the value, sanctity, and authority of the truth. The bright beams of heaven's light are shining upon your pathway, dear youth, and I pray that you may make the most of your opportunities. Receive and cherish every heaven-sent ray, and your path will grow brighter and brighter unto the perfect day" (*Youth's Instructor*, Feb. 2, 1893).

Sharing Time

You can share the principles you have learned about decision-making with your friends. Show them that the Bible is a good guide to help them make decisions. Remember that the Bible, prayer, and peace can be great guides.

Consider This

Look at Gideon's method of obtaining direction in Judges 6:36-40. Look at chapter 53 of *Patriarchs and Prophets* to see what Ellen White shares about Gideon's choice. How can you apply this to your life this week?

Divorce

how to live with your parents' choice

This study is specifically for those dealing with divorce and separation in the family. The young people may be living with a custodial parent, part-time with both parents, and possibly dealing with stepparents. Feelings may run full circle with this topic. Remember to pray for your young people—divorce hurts everyone.

Icebreaker

He walked along an unseen trail through the jungle. Noises filled the air with a cacophony of sound that drove him further toward insanity. The loneliness was beginning to wear on what was left of his nerves. One wrong move was all it would take, and his life could be over in seconds. A snake slid across the path, its tail the last visible mark in the sand. A monkey called from high above. He marked his path with the shreds of his shirt, which he carried tightly. He turned at the sound and sank chest-deep into the sand. As he cried out, no one could hear his plea as the sand sucked him farther into its grasp.

Quicksand! Well, not exactly. The scene above has been repeated thousands of times on the big screen, but in real life quicksand is not the monster of movie lore.

Quicksand is rarely more than a few feet deep; it certainly cannot swallow a human whole in its bottomless pit. So what is it and how would you get out if you ever did fall into its clutches?

Quicksand is literally sand that has been oversaturated by water. Some sort of agitation has lifted the grains away from each other, and the material begins to behave in a liquidlike manner. This saturation actually makes the sand float on top of the water. It is a messy-looking mixture, and its density is about twice that of the human body.

The best way to get out is to float—literally. Use slow movements, because exciting the material causes more suction as the friction packs the grains closer together. Don't panic, go slow, and float. Those are the keys to getting out of quicksand.

Dig In

Another Hollywood myth is invading families. Somehow the marriages on the big screen work out happily ever after, but it's just not true in the real world. The facts are in and they tell a sad story. Divorce occurs nearly as much in Christian families as it does in the world at large. And that hurts everyone involved, especially the most vulnerable members of the family: the children, regardless of their age.

When divorce happens, everything changes. And the change is seldom good for the children. That's why God says that He doesn't like divorce. Marriage was established in Eden, and it was designed to be a lifelong companionship between a man and a woman—a relationship that would eventually include children. Because of sin, and with it the desires of the human heart gone awry, God permits divorce for reasons of adultery and what it entails. But God's ideal choice is that we try to reconcile—to forgive and be forgiven, to change our behavior so that a marriage can be salvaged and a new beginning made. But what happens when that doesn't happen or can't happen?

Hot Potato

Just as there are stages in the grieving process of losing a loved one, there are stages most people go through when facing and living with a divorce. These happen in the lives of all people in the relationship—even the children.

The first stage is survival. The single parent now has the responsibility of paying bills on only one income. That puts demands on their time, which affects the children in the marriage too. Instead of the work being divided, it is now taken on by one. The children may have more chores or none at all. So what can you do? It is important that you, as young people, help your parents. You don't have to become the resident Cinderella, but helping doesn't hurt anyone. And it can help your relationship as you show you can handle responsibility.

The second stage is often grief. As the separation widens the family, sadness and loss set in. For young people, this can cause all kinds of symptoms of a very real pain. With youth, it can cause ideas of suicide, depression, and violent anger. While you may feel alone, you aren't. If you are having trouble, it is imperative that you find help from a trusted adult. You may also wonder if you will be able to have a lasting relationship yourself when the time comes. With God's help you can. But for now, don't suffer alone. Ask a youth pastor or other adult to help you. You don't have to go through grief alone.

The third stage is about identity. Some call this the "crazy stage." It is a time of discovery, and that can be good. But often it is more about acting out in ways that have the potential for being harmful. Adults and young people often go through this stage. It is important to identify why you want to try something new—and make sure your motives are good. You don't have anything to prove—to others, or to yourself.

The last stage is about direction. This is the stage that helps you to feel more comfortable with the new situation and plan for the future. It is like acceptance in grieving and having the will to pick up and start again. It is the stage that helps you to heal in a positive way. It's the stage of forgiveness—something that is near and dear to your heavenly Father's heart. It is His act of reconciliation that helps us to forgive.

Hot Potato Questions

- If you are going through a breakup in your family, how are you supposed to feel?
- Does God still love you if you are angry? if you are bitter? if you are disappointed?
- Is it hard to show respect for one or both of your parents? Why is it harder to respect one more than the other?
- Do you feel that your right to choose has been taken away from you by the courts and lawyers? by your parents?
- Have your grades suffered as a result of divorce in your family? Why do you think that could happen?
- Do you feel as though you are put in the middle? Do you feel that you can refuse to take a side?
- How can you still maintain love and respect for both of your parents? How about respecting stepparents? Is that something you are able to do? Why or why not?

Bible Discovery

Exodus 20:12. The Bible tells us to honor our parents. Is it harder to do this when your parents have chosen to divorce? Why or why not? If you have stepparents, should that respect extend to them? Why do you feel this way? Is it harder to respect your parents or your stepparents? Why? Do you think God wants you to choose to respect your parents even if their behavior might not support respect? Should you ever do anything that comes between you and God? (See also Colossians 3:21.)

Proverbs 1:8. Do your parents always have wise advice for you? Can their struggle with divorce change the parenting patterns you are used to? Why do you think that might be? Should you listen to each of them and try to find a compromise that will help all of you? If you spend time with your parents, could you possibly begin to understand them better and be able to see their struggle? Have your parents been through a lot, and can they pass that knowledge on to you if you let them?

Psalm 103:13. Does God have compassion for what you are going through? Do you know that your parents love you? Can that love help you understand how much God loves you? Love needs to be validated. Can you offer your heavenly Father's compassion to your parents? Can you still share a hug with your parents? Even when things are at their worst, can you pray for your family and yourself?

Proverbs 3:11, 12. Is it harder to be disciplined by your parents since they have gone through a divorce? Why do you think that is? Is discipline a sign of anger and resentment or can it be a sign of love? Does God use discipline to help us grow into the beautiful people He wants us to become? When your parents discipline you—including stepparents—how do you feel? Do you think God understands you?

Malachi 2:13-16. What does God say about divorce? Why do you think He hates divorce so much? Why do you think He permits divorce for reasons of adultery? Does divorce hurt God? Is divorce forgivable by a loving God? Do we need to find forgiveness in order to be whole?

Does that mean that we also need to extend forgiveness? Is that always easy to do? Why or why not? What can you do to help you come to the point where you can forgive?

EXTRA GEM

Ellen White gave wise counsel to a couple contemplating divorce. Read what she wrote and let it help to encourage you when you seek to have a complete marriage: "A husband and wife should cultivate respect and affection for each other. They should guard the spirit, the words, and the actions so that nothing will be said or done to irritate or annoy. Each is to have a care for the other, doing all in their power to strengthen their mutual affection. I tell you both to seek the Lord. In love and kindness do your duty one to the other. The husband should cultivate industrious habits, doing his best to support his family. This will lead his wife to have respect for him. . . . My sister, you cannot please God by maintaining your present attitude. Forgive your husband. He is your husband, and you will be blessed in striving to be a dutiful, affectionate wife. Let the law of kindness be on your lips. You can and must change your attitude. You must both study how you can assimilate, instead of differing, with one another. . . . The use of mild, gentle methods will make a surprising difference in your lives" (*The Adventist Home*, p. 345).

Sharing Time

Read Matthew 7:1. What does it say about judging others? You may be going through a rough time with your parents' divorce. You are not appointed to be their judge. What can you do to offer forgiving love? Think of simple gestures that will show your parents that you love them still.

Consider This

Remember that God loves you! He loved you before your parents' divorce, and He still loves you now. You can depend on Him. Find your favorite verse of comfort and memorize it. Then when you are feeling especially vulnerable, you can say it out loud, and it will help you to be assured of your Father's love and comfort.

Ecology
taking care of creation

This is a self-contained Bible study. It is good for individuals as well as groups. There is nothing to prepare ahead of time. You might want to find recycling statistics for your country if they are not listed.

Icebreaker

Do you love mountains? Do you like to hike trails? Then there is a little-known spot that you might not have heard of. At more than 1,000 feet above sea level it could provide you with a little hiking exercise. The fact that you can find cheap hotel rates in the area might be a draw. There's more than 500 acres to explore. Want to visit? The area offers free tours on Wednesdays. And they even provide transportation for the tour. How can you pass up a deal like that?

You might want to rethink that.

Mount Rumpke is in the state of Ohio. Except that it's not a true mountain in any sense. It is a landfill. It is one of the largest landfills in the U.S. What started in 1945 grows by 2 million tons of industrial and household waste annually. In 2005 it expanded by 300 acres. But you better hurry if you want to take that tour. It is expected to be full by 2022!

But if you are in the U.S., don't worry. There are more than 13,000 such landfills quite "ripe" for an adventure.

The largest landfill in the world isn't even on land. It's called the Great Pacific Garbage Patch, and it sits in the northern Pacific Ocean. It's really two areas: the first is twice the size of Texas, and floats between Hawaii and California; the second is east of Japan and west of Hawaii. Ninety percent of it is plastic, which accounts for about 10 percent of the world's plastic waste! These landfills cause many hazards to marine life, fishing, and tourism.

What are we doing to our world?

Dig In

When God created Adam and Eve, He made them stewards of the earth. God gave Adam rule over the earth to subdue it. (See Genesis 1:26-28.) Does that mean that people can exploit the earth? What do you think

God had in mind? Remember that this command was given before the fall of humanity. Does that change the perspective?

As Christians, there are so many things that need our attention. Do we have a responsibility to also think about the environment? Is taking care of the earth someone else's responsibility?

Hot Potato

It has become increasingly popular to view God as part of nature. This is the New Age view you might be acquainted with. It is also called pantheism. It views all nature as equal because God is in all of nature. It puts a human equal with a blade of grass. It literally means "God is all" and "All is God." Do you think that this is what God intended for us? Why or why not? Part of the belief of pantheism is that there are many gods. Does that help clarify the issue?

God (notice the big G) is the Creator of nature, not part of nature. Nature has value because God created it. If we look, we can find God's character in nature. Look at the perfectly formed petals of a flower. See how patterns are repeated over and over. Look close to see how a slice of cauliflower looks just like part of the cerebellum—the part of the brain that controls movement. Look up! See God's amazing character in the night sky.

Hot Potato Questions
- Do you think that the New Age movement is entirely wrong? Aren't they at least worshipping God?
- Is ecology something that really matters in your Christian life?
- Is it something you can let others figure out? After all, things aren't in jeopardy within your lifetime, right?

Bible Discovery
Romans 1:18-20. Do you accept that God is the Creator of all the world? Do you believe that God has made His character plain to us in nature? Why or why not? Does this verse leave humanity without excuse for finding God—even without the Bible? Do you know that God is the Creator of nature and not part of nature?

Genesis 1:27. God created humanity. Whose image were they formed in? Is any other created thing made in the image of God? Does the fact that we were created in God's image separate us from other creation?

Genesis 2:15. Humans were put in the Garden of Eden. But what work did God give to them? Adam and Eve were eventually removed from the Garden of Eden because of sin. Did God then exempt them from taking care of the earth?

Psalm 104. David talks about the wonder and majesty of God's creation. He shows how God takes care of even the animals. If God cares about the animals and the earth He created, shouldn't we care about it too?

Matthew 6:26. This scripture tells us that God cares even for the smallest of the birds. How does that relate to us caring for the earth? Do we have a responsibility as Christians to protect the earth for all of God's creation? Or are we responsible only for caring for our needs? Explain why you feel the way you do.

Isaiah 5:8-10. What warning did God give to the people in Isaiah's time about building up large estates while robbing the land of its intended use? Do you think these same principles apply today?

EXTRA GEM

Ellen White understood how people have been led to believe that God was nature. She wrote about it in an article in *Christian Educator,* April 1, 1899: "The voice of nature testifies of God, declaring His glory; but nature itself is not God. As God's created work, it but bears a testimony of His power."

In the same article she also wrote: "Those who have a true knowledge of God will not become so infatuated with the laws of matter and the operations of nature as to overlook or to refuse to acknowledge the continual working of God in nature. Deity is the author of nature. The natural world has in itself no inherent power but that which God supplies. How strange, then, that so many make a deity of nature! God furnishes the matter and the properties with which to carry out His plans. Nature is but His agency."

Sharing Time

Romans 8:22 tells us that "we know that the whole creation has been groaning as in the pains of childbirth right up to the present time" (NIV). Why is nature groaning? Is it waiting for its restoration into its original perfection?

Share the story of Creation from God's Word with your friends. Help them understand that sin has caused the ruin of our planet. Sin was the choice of mankind, and we have been continuing our bad choices ever since. But it is time to start making better choices for the world that God has left in our care. We know that the world will be restored. We too will be restored into the perfect creation that God designed us to be, a reflection of His image! What better news can you share with others?

Consider This

Do you recycle?

The United States, which makes up about 5 percent of the world's population, produces 30 percent of the world's waste, more than any other nation, but recycles only about 30 percent.

Austria recycles about 50 percent of its waste. Greece recycles about 20 percent of its waste.

The United Kingdom, Ireland, Italy, and Portugal recycle about 18 percent of their waste products. Singapore recycles nearly 60 percent of its waste, with the ultimate target of zero landfill use.

Do you recycle? Where does your country fit into the picture? Find out about recycling in your area. Start small, and if you aren't already recycling, start. Any effort is better than none. Plastics, glass, and paper are the easiest items to recycle. Another method you might want to try is precycling, which means not buying things that can't be reused, such as plastic wrap and products with plastic rings. Doing both will help reduce garbage and help keep the earth clean.

Eschatology and Prophecies
the promises of God

This study is meant to show young people that the Bible and God are true to their word. God is faithful and we can depend on Him. What He says will happen—will happen. It's this being able to depend on Him that gives our future hope. Even with everything around us going crazy, we can depend on the promises and prophecies of God!

Icebreaker

It was one of the scares of the century. And it was only a few years ago. With the dawning of the year 2000, it was thought that the world's computer system would crash. Why? As you know, you who are more computer literate than any generation before you, your computer system updates itself on time and date automatically. To save storage space, computer programmers had built only a two-digit year system into most computers. So no one knew what would happen when systems rolled over to 2000, or 00. Would they think it was the year 1000? 1900? Would computers crash? Would nuclear weapons launch themselves and cause mass destruction?

The problem was that no one knew exactly what would happen. They could theorize. They could run tests. But in the computer world such a problem comes around only every 100 years, and since there weren't computers back in the late 1800s, the problem had never occurred before.

Many people chose to ignore the situation and let things play out as they would. Others chose to do things such as stock up on food and other necessities, fearing crashing computers would stifle such things as banking, cash registers, transportation . . . well, just about everything, since our world literally runs on computers. Many claimed special prophecies for the time. They predicted everything from world war to world destruction.

The time came. Everyone waited to see what would happen. Kiritimati came first. Haven't heard of it? It's part of an island group just past the international date line. It's part of the Line Islands, which are part of the Republic of Kiribati. The islands are not far from New Zealand. Approximately 5,000 residents started the celebration as the world watched. As the day progressed across continents and oceans, and computers didn't crash, people around the world celebrated—and had to think about what they were going to do with all those perishable things they had stored up just in case!

So much for the prophets of doom!

Dig In

The world has always had prophets. Humanity has always wanted to know what was to come—what would the future bring to our ever-expanding world? We know that many so-called prophets have failed the test of time. Their predictions have not come true. Others have had some success, but many of their prophecies have been general. The most accurate prophecies, of course, are found in the Bible. Yet even there, false prophets are recorded, along with their failed predictions. But God's prophets were given their visions from God, and since He can see the future, they have been 100 percent accurate.

Hot Potato

Why is prophecy so important, and what does it teach us about God?

Prophecy simply means a prediction of the future. Where the Bible is concerned, it means that the revelation of the prophecy came from God Himself. Why is prophecy important to us as Christians? Do we need to know the future? While the gift of prophecy does give us an inkling into the future, it also shows us that God is irrefutable. His character is never-changing. His promises are dependable. His love is unmatchable. What He says will happen—will happen. He is the alpha and the omega, the beginning and the end. Prophecy, among other things, lets us know that we have a God who can be trusted. Did prophets of other gods in Bible times predict things? Sure they did. Did they come true? Not at all. So everyone feared and respected the Bible prophets, right? After all, what they said came true if it was from God. No to that one, too. Even Jesus said that a prophet got no respect in their hometown. (See Matthew 13:57.) So why are prophecies and prophets important to us?

Hot Potato Questions

- After sin, what prophecy was given to the people that was filled with promise? (Leaders, point out that Jesus was the prophecy that gave us a Savior.)
- Was this prophecy fulfilled? By whom? Why was this particular

prophecy important to the people living in Old Testament times? Why is the fulfillment of this prophecy important in our time?

- Did Jesus predict things that were to happen in the future? Could we be living in those times? Why do you think the way you do? Does Bible prophecy scare you, or is it exciting, or a mixture of both?
- Should we fear the Bible's predictions of the future? Why or why not?
- Should knowing that all Bible prophecy has so far been 100 percent accurate tell you that you can trust God for the future?
- Does end-time prophecy set a date for Christ's second coming? Why do you think that is?
- Do you think that Jesus could return during your lifetime? Explain why you believe as you do.

Bible Discovery

2 Peter 1:21; Amos 3:7; Ephesians 4:8-15; Jeremiah 28:8, 9. What is the origin of all prophecy? Who works with God to show people what they are to say and do? Why do you think God reveals Himself through prophecy? What can we learn about God's character as a result of His revelation through prophecy? Is prophecy a gift? What things will prophecy do for us? How will we know if a prophet is from the Lord? What does Jeremiah 28:9 give as a simple test of truth?

Isaiah 7:14; Isaiah 9:1-7; Isaiah 53. What "sign" was given about the Savior? Was the fact that He was born of a virgin significant? Why do you think this way? From the prophecy in Isaiah 9, where was the Messiah's first work to take place? Did Jesus begin His work in Galilee? The titles given to Jesus in Isaiah 9:6 have both a human and divine component. How do these describe Jesus? Are they accurate? Was Jesus God's Son? Yet, was He, like prophets before Him, rejected by His own people? Do the verses in Isaiah 53 accurately describe Jesus' life and death and burial while He was on the earth? Would it have been possible for someone to know these prophecies and "arrange" them to make out that He was the true Messiah? Why or why not?

Isaiah 61:1-3; Luke 4:16-21. What does Isaiah prophesy about Jesus many years before He was born? Can prophecies have dual meaning—a fulfillment in the time and the fulfillment at a later time? Why do you think this way? Is this a prophecy of Jesus' mission in coming to the earth?

Is there another mission that will happen with His second coming? How do you think the people in the Temple felt when Jesus read the words from Isaiah? Do you think they were hoping that He was the fulfillment? Do you think it helped many to believe? Do you think it angered some? What a blessing it must have been to be there that day and hear the Messiah read the words written about Him between 1043 B.C. and 973 B.C.

Joel 2:29-32; Matthew 24. What can we learn from the verses in Joel? Does this describe the time just before Jesus comes the second time? Does the Bible say that there will be prophesying in the last days? Does God count time differently than we do? Does Bible prophecy give us the hope that we can indeed be saved and part of God's kingdom because Jesus came as was foretold? Does Mathew 24 teach that there will be false prophets and teachers in the end days? If there are false prophets and teachers, does that imply that there will be true prophets and teachers? Which prophet was Jesus' contemporary and taught about His coming? Was what John the Baptist taught fulfilled? Could it be that God will send a prophet before His second coming to help make the way clearer for His people? Could this prophet be Ellen G. White? Why do you feel this way? If the Bible tells us that something is going to happen, can we trust and believe that it will happen? Do you feel that way? Do you believe that Jesus, the Son of God, came once to save you and will return soon to redeem you for eternity?

EXTRA GEM

Ellen White encourages us to study and read the final book of prophecy. Read what she writes: "In the Revelation are portrayed the deep things of God. The very name given to its inspired pages, 'the Revelation,' contradicts the statement that this is a sealed book. A revelation is something revealed. The Lord Himself revealed to His servant the mysteries contained in this book, and He designs that they shall be open to the study of all. Its truths are addressed to those living in the last days of this earth's history, as well as to those living in the days of John. Some of the scenes depicted in this prophecy are in the past, some are now taking place; some bring to view the close of the great conflict between the powers of darkness and the Prince of heaven, and some reveal the triumphs and joys of the redeemed in the earth made new. Let none think, because they cannot explain the meaning of every symbol in the Revelation, that it is useless for them to search this book in an effort to know the meaning of the truth it contains. The One who revealed these mysteries to John will give to the diligent searcher for truth a foretaste of heavenly things. Those whose hearts are open to the reception of truth will be enabled to understand its teachings, and will be granted the blessing promised to those who 'hear the words of this prophecy, and keep those things which are written therein'" (*The Acts of the Apostles*, p. 584).

Sharing Time

It's not only Christians that realize something big is happening in the world we live in. Others, outside of God's family, recognize that somebody is in control of this world, and that it must soon end. How can you encourage others to study Scripture to see that the Bible prophecies are accurate? Make a list of some of the prophecies that even history records as being fulfilled and be ready to present them to nonbelievers. The proof is in the Bible for all to see.

Consider This

Psalm 22 is a special psalm that prophesies 11 different things about Jesus' crucifixion. Take the time to read it through and see if you can find all 11 examples of how this prophecy was fulfilled in Jesus' death on Calvary. Make sure to mark your Bible with the New Testament texts that show them being fulfilled.

Fear

facing challenges in life

Review the lesson and understand that teens face many challenges, including fears that they do not yet have the experience to handle. Be prepared for them to share some of their greatest fears. If they are willing to talk, be willing to listen!

Icebreaker

Birding may not be your thing, but there are some very important lessons that we can all learn from birds. Having raised cockatiels, we learned quite a few of these lessons. One came on a day just before Christmas. Since our pair of cockatiels decided to go into the birdie business on their own, we were blessed with several sets of babies. Some we gave away, and some we sold. This particular time a family had just come to pick out the baby they wanted as a gift. They left him in our care until Christmas Eve.

We did not always clip our birds' wings, so we often let them out to get a little exercise and to play with them. Letting them out wasn't hard to do at all. If you left the cage door open, it wasn't long before they saw the chance for freedom and escaped. Getting them back was the hard part. On this particular day, all were back in the aviary except for the one we had just sold. He was being very stubborn. After several long minutes of wild flight, he finally settled on the curtain rod to take a break. His little heart was beating fast. Our son reached up to grab him and put him back, but managed only to snag his tail.

The bird took off, leaving all of its tail feathers in our son's hand. The beautiful bird we had just sold was now something quite smaller and pretty silly looking.

What we didn't know was that God put this instinct into birds. Just like some reptiles, birds can drop their tails and escape when threatened. Often the tail is the largest part of the bird, so that is what predators go after to nab them. Sometimes it is the heaviest part, so dropping it will enable the bird to flee quickly.

The feathers grow back, and our little birdie's did too. But what a lesson we learned. If God made a way for birds to escape danger, how much more will He do for us?

Dig In

Fear is a terrible thing—most of the time. It can paralyze us, and it can hold us back from being all that we were meant to be. It robs us of things that God intended for us to enjoy, such as joy, peace, and destiny. It saps us of self-confidence and can alter our self-esteem. Yet fear is something we must all face in our lives. Teens, especially, have to deal with major fear without the experience to know how to handle it. Have you ever felt that way?

Just as it was when the Hebrews came running out of Egypt, fear of the unknown can be paralyzing. Change is something that is difficult even for adults to handle. Sometimes it just seems easier to go back to our old ways—places where we were comfortable—even if those ways were harmful and destructive. The Hebrews faced the waters of the sea on one side and a pursuing army on the other. Talk about being caught between a rock and a hard place. So it is easy to see why they were afraid. They hadn't yet developed their faith enough to trust that God would deliver them. Have you ever felt as though you were caught between a rock and a hard place too?

Hot Potato
Becoming Silver—Malachi 3:3
For silver to be valuable, it must be pure. But purifying silver is not an easy process. To refine the silver, the silversmith must hold it raw in fire. And not just any fire—it takes a very hot fire to purify silver. The silversmith must sit and put the raw material into the very hottest part of the fire. Only then can impurities such as dirt and other things be burned away.

Have you ever felt like God was letting you stay in a hot place?

While the silversmith is doing all this, they never leave the silver. They sit in front of the fire and watch it very carefully. If they leave it for even a moment too long in the fire, it can be destroyed.

God doesn't leave you when you are in the fire!

The silversmith knows that silver is purified when they can see their image in it. That's what God wants for us—to be made into His image.

Fear is something common in the world today. With war, famine, and terrorism as daily threats, it is only natural to be afraid. But do we have to? Do you have to be afraid of all the things going on around you?

Hot Potato Questions
- Do you ever wish that God wouldn't put you "through the fire"?
- Is it ever too much for you to handle?

• Is God big enough to handle all your fears? Are you sure of your answer?

Bible Discovery

Isaiah 43:1. When you were created in your mother's womb, who knew you then? Did the Creator who named you promise He would redeem you? If God knows you so intimately, can you trust Him with your fears? Do you fear failure? You may act like you don't care when something happens, but deep inside, you do care more than you let on. If your self-esteem is hurt, is it easy to "bounce back"? Can you trust God to help you let your fear of failure go?

Psalm 118:6, 7. David feared disappointing God. Do you ever feel that way? It is hard enough when you disappoint yourself, but it can be worse when you realize you have to deal with disappointing others, as well. Do you get angry with yourself for doing this? Do you feel as if God won't like you if you disappoint Him? David felt that way too, but then he turned his fears over to God and realized that the Lord was always with him and that He was his helper in all things—including conquering his fears. Can you grow to feel that way too?

2 Timothy 1:7. What does this verse tell you about how God has called you to be? What does timidity mean? (Leaders, you may need to explain this to your youth, or have them look it up in a dictionary.) Do you fear being misunderstood? Do you want others to like you because of the way you dress? Do you fear your parent will overreact to something you have done? Do you want others to know who you really are, but are confused because you don't always know that yourself? Does power work well with love? What can love do that will help us with our fears?

1 John 4:18. There is no fear in love. Do you accept that? How can love drive out fear? What does perfect love have for us? Do you ever fear those you love because you have done something you feel you should be punished for? Have you ever been given grace as a result of love?

John 14:27; Romans 5:1, 2. How can you feel peace through your fears? Is surrendering them to God the only way to get real peace? Is this easy or hard because of human nature? Why do you feel this way? Peace is a gift that God offers freely. Is it effective only when we accept this gift? Will you choose to do that today?

EXTRA GEM

Listen to this promise that Ellen White shares about fear:

"Fear Brings No Relief to the Soul—You should have a clear apprehension of the gospel. The religious life is not one of gloom and of sadness but of peace and joy coupled with Christlike dignity and holy solemnity. We are not encouraged by our Savior to cherish doubts and fears and distressing forebodings; these bring no relief to the soul and should be rebuked rather than praised. We may have joy unspeakable and full of glory" (manuscript 6, 1888; *Evangelism,* p. 180; *Mind, Character, and Personality,* vol. 2, p. 476).

Sharing Time

There are many things we can do to help others with their fears. One of the best we can do is to be a good listener. This week, take time to listen to your friends as they express their fears, and remind them that Jesus wants to carry their burdens. We just have to choose to let Him. Did you know that "fear not" appears in the Bible 365 times—one for each day of the year. Our God is so good!

Consider This

One of the most effective ways to deal with fear is to memorize Scripture. Take the challenge of memorizing at least one text this week that you can draw on to help you with your fears. Luke 12:22-26 is a wonderful place to start!

Forgiveness

chasing your tail

Leaders, the cost of forgiveness is priceless, literally. Our forgiveness cost the life of God's own Son. Forgiving others not only changes their lives—it changes ours. Though it is sometimes hard to do, it is always worth the cost. Remind your youth that forgiveness isn't the same as accepting abuse. You can forgive but may have to make a choice to put someone out of your life for your own safety. Young people need to learn to forgive, and you get the chance to help them. Lucky you!

Icebreaker

Can you believe that someone has taken the time to measure how far hamsters run in their wheels at night? And the record is six miles. But statistics say that some rodents can run much farther. In 24 hours a rat can run 26 miles (42 kilometers). Now, if you are a field mouse, those little legs can propel you about 18.5 miles (30 kilometers). Don't ever underestimate the power of little things!

Scientists have also studied why hamsters run in their wheels and what kinds of wheels they like. The most likely reason is they enjoy exercise. At least, that is the most likely answer. Some theorize that animals get a high off of running, like some people do who run for fun. And it seems the bigger the wheel, the happier the rodent. So remember that the next time you visit your local pet store.

Humans have their own version of the hamster wheel. The treadmill dates back much earlier than its rodent counterpart. The first treadmill appeared around 1875, but it wasn't built for humans. It was designed for animal power, actually. The energy harnessed was used to operate things such as butter churns and spinning wheels. The largest of these was run by horses and used to operate threshing machines. In the 1920s the technology came to factories, where it cut the cost of labor so much that it made previously unattainable luxuries affordable to more of society. (Think automobiles.) Then in 1952 a physician named Robert Bruce took the technology and began using it for stress tests. By the 1960s the treadmill had become a standard piece of equipment in gyms and homes, and it still is today.

Dig In

Do you ever feel as if you are a hamster on a wheel—or on an endless treadmill? Do you feel as though sometimes you take two steps forward for every three steps back? If you do, you are certainly not alone. We seem to like being part of a perpetual cycle of frustration.

Humans seem to have invented a whole new lifestyle out of chasing their own tail, much like the hamster. And we seem to bring that tail-chasing activity into many areas of our lives, such as forgiveness.

Hot Potato

Did you know that there are dangers for the little creatures forced to run on their hamster wheels? That's been documented too. Veterinarians see many injuries to these animals every year. It is estimated that a hamster has about a 70 percent chance of sustaining injuries because of wheel running. These injuries include such things as broken feet, legs, tails, and toes. Sometimes they even get crushed between the cage and the wheel.

What happens when a pet rodent gets injured? There are really only three choices: let it die slowly (we won't talk about how painful this is), euthanization, or pay to have surgery. Be forewarned, hamster foot amputations go for about US$1,500!

We run risks too when it comes to chasing our tails. Besides wearing ourselves out, when we bring tail-chasing into other areas of our lives, we have a huge chance of causing painful damage. Especially when it comes to forgiveness. The Bible tells us to forgive others. That sometimes isn't so easy to do. But the hardest part of forgiving doesn't even involve someone else—it's between you and God. And quite often we ask for forgiveness for the same problem again and again because we don't feel like we are worthy of accepting it.

It is hard for us as humans to believe that God can forgive and forget, because that is very difficult for us to do. But He can and does! When we ask for forgiveness, God forgives. It's really that simple. Jesus' death on the cross assures us of that. The problem lies in accepting that forgiveness—a task that often puts us back on the treadmill of life chasing our tails. It's often easy to forgive someone, but very difficult to accept that we have been forgiven.

Why is it so hard to accept God's forgiveness? Some people have never experienced forgiveness from their parents, friends, or other family members. Others may have experienced conditional forgiveness—forgiveness that depends on an "if," or with constant reminders of the past. Still others have a difficult time because they don't see the need to be forgiven.

Hot Potato Questions
- So why do you think it is so hard for us to accept God's forgiveness?
- Ask yourself, "How do my attitudes and beliefs contribute to this cycle of frustration?"

Bible Discovery
1 John 1:8, 9. It is human nature to want to deny our wrongdoings. But the Bible makes it clear that we are all sinners, and that we all need to seek forgiveness. God is love, and in that love He doesn't force anything on anyone. We are free to choose. Do you think you need to ask for and accept His forgiveness? Is there a part of this you find difficult to do?

Romans 5:8. Wait a minute! What did that verse say? When did God accept us? He loved us while we were still sinners. Is that hard to accept? Accepting His forgiveness must come from our hearts. How do you feel about this?

Isaiah 59:1, 2. Unforgiven sin separates us from God. It hurts our relationship with Him. We need to ask for forgiveness and accept it if we want to have a relationship with the Father, who loves us beyond our understanding! Do you agree with this?

Matthew 6:12-15. We are told in these familiar verses that we *must* forgive others. Is it a matter of choice? If we want to be forgiven, do we have to forgive? It may not be easy, but God will help us if we ask. That is a promise. Do you know that God keeps His promises? Is it easy for you to forgive others? (See also Ephesians 4:32 and 1 Corinthians 13:5.)

Psalm 32:1, 2; Isaiah 43:25; Psalm 103:12. What happens when we forgive and are forgiven? Will we be blessed and have true happiness? God says that He won't remember our sins, and He says that He will remove them from us. No more sin! Can you trust God to forgive and forget?

Philippians 3:13, 14. We know we must forgive others and that God forgives us. So what is the last step? Is it learning to accept God's forgiveness? Paul understood this challenge. He held the coats of those stoning Stephen. He had some weighty things to be forgiven for. It is our choice to accept God's unmerited favor. We may not deserve it, but God offers it. It is a gift. Like any gift, does it have to be opened to enjoy it? God loves you! Can you learn to accept this? Do you think it can help you find freedom?

EXTRA GEM

Ellen White shares what God showed her about forgiving in the following quote: "We are not forgiven *because* we forgive, but *as* we forgive. The ground of all forgiveness is found in the unmerited love of God, but by our attitude toward others we show whether we have made that love our own. Wherefore Christ says, 'With what judgment ye judge, ye shall be judged; and with what measure ye mete, it shall be measured to you again' (Matt. 7:2)" (*Christ's Object Lessons,* p. 251).

Sharing Time

Many people wonder what blasphemy of the Holy Spirit is. Maybe your friends have talked about it before. The Holy Spirit's job is to convict us of sin. When He works with us our consciences can be convicted of sin. But if we continually push Him away, how will we be reminded of sin and the need to ask for forgiveness? This week, help your friends understand what the Holy Spirit's job is and why the Holy Spirit is so important in our lives. Remind them of God's grace and the need to forgive as we are forgiven. (See John 16:7-10.)

Consider This

David understood the need for forgiveness of sin. Read Psalm 51:10-12. Can you ask God—like David did—for a pure heart? When we are right with God, we too will be filled with the joy that only salvation brings.

Forgiving Others

accepting God's forgiveness

One of the hardest things for young people to accept is forgiveness. They haven't yet learned how to completely forgive others, and the idea of being truly forgiven is even harder for them to grasp. But God's forgiveness is complete. Learning about this will help them to grow leaps and bounds in their personal relationship with a very personal God.

Icebreaker

They've been in existence for thousands of years in South America. The Incas ground them into paste, and they've been found in the tombs of mummies in Peru. They are small, but the world could hardly live without them. Their flavor blends with African stew, Chinese cooking, and of course, chocolate. What are we talking about? Peanuts, of course.

Their migration as a food crop probably took the route of South America to Africa to Europe, then on to other parts of the world. But George Washington Carver made them the focus of his research at Alabama's Tuskegee Institute in 1903, and there he found more than 300 uses for the little nugget.

In the 1890s a doctor in St. Louis, Missouri, went looking for an affordable source of protein for his poorer patients who had lost their teeth and couldn't chew meat. He experimented with grinding the small nuts into a paste. The idea was taken to George A. Bayle, Jr., the owner of a food company that soon began producing the paste and selling it for a mere six cents a pound. At the same time, Dr. John Harvey Kellogg, physician at the famed Battle Creek Sanitarium in Battle Creek, Michigan, began experimenting with the peanut paste himself. He was looking for a source of protein for his patients who wanted to explore a vegetarian diet. It was Dr. Kellogg who eventually was awarded the patent for peanut butter.

Peanut butter made its public debut at the 1904 St. Louis World Fair, and it was a hit! The concession stand sold more than $700 at the fair—and the desire for this wonderful, nutty butter was born!

The peanut isn't actually a nut at all. It's a legume and part of the pea family. Grown underground, peanuts are still a widely grown crop in South America. Americans spend $800 million a year on peanut butter. So however you use them, peanuts have worked their way into the diets of the world, and sometimes you know, you've just got to have some!

Dig In

So next time you are snacking on that peanut butter-and-jelly sandwich, think about this. Peanut butter is known for its sticky properties. That's one of the reasons it is so usable in cooking. Try eating it when you have a dry mouth, and you'll no doubt agree—peanut butter is sticky. Some of the most important things in the world are sticky, such as spiderwebs, honey, mud, and glue. Sticky things have their purpose.

Some biblical concepts tend to be sticky for us, too. And that includes some of the most important ones. One of them—forgiveness—can be one of the stickiest for most people. Why is it so sticky? Because it is one of the hardest concepts for us to wrap ourselves around.

God forgives you when you ask! But try telling that to someone who has done something really wrong. It's just hard to accept that a perfect God would let you off the hook so easily. It's not that you aren't held responsible, but the guilt can be taken away. It's even difficult when you do something that doesn't seem so bad, but you know you shouldn't have done it. Your conscience works overtime, often telling you your sin can't be forgiven. It's not your conscience at all; it's more than likely the one who wants to make your sins as sticky as peanut butter. But God has the solution. You just have to trust Him.

Hot Potato

The problem really kicks in when someone does something to you. Maybe it's really bad, maybe it's not, but how will you ever get over the hurt and betrayal? That's the stickiness again. Forgive them? You've got to be kidding! But that's exactly what the Bible says we have to do. So maybe you'll decide to forgive but not forget. That's a good solution, right?

Hot Potato Questions
- How would you define forgiveness?
- Can you forgive and not forget? Why or why not?
- Does God forgive and forget? How do you know this? What is the easiest for you: to accept God's forgiveness or to forgive others?
- Does God's forgiveness give us the power to forgive others? How are we forgiven by God? What was the cost of this forgiveness?

- If you have never experienced forgiveness from others—parents, family, and friends—can you learn to accept God's forgiveness? Would it be more difficult?
- How can you get past the stickiness of forgiving—and learn to practice forgiving others?

Bible Discovery

Luke 23:34. These are Jesus' words from the cross about the very people who put Him there. Do you think they are reflective of God's character? Jesus was concerned about His enemies even while in the grip of death. God's answer to forgiveness is easy—it's the cross! Can you accept God's forgiveness? Can you learn to forgive others as Jesus did? Is this a matter of just head work or heart work?

John 16:7-9. What are some of the responsibilities of the Holy Spirit? Who alone has the power to convict of sin? Is the Holy Spirit our conscience? Will the Holy Spirit continue to remind us of our sin once it is forgiven? Why is it important that we accept forgiveness and live forgiven? What does it say to God when we refuse His grace?

Isaiah 43:25. How long does God remember our sins? Does He write them down and think about them at night? When He looks down at you in the morning, do you think He says, "Yep. There he/she is. I remember two years ago when . . ."? Of course you think that's silly! God says that if we ask, He will forgive. But do we do the same for others? How many times do you say, "Yep. There he/she is. I remember two years ago when . . ."? Do you think that's fair in light of how God treats us?

1 Corinthians 13:5. Love is being described in this verse. Perfect love. Do you think that God loves you with perfect love? If this is part of God's character—to forgive and forget—shouldn't we try to be more like our Father? Should we let God forgive us? Can we accept that forgiveness? Can we in turn forgive others? Can you learn to forgive yourself? Which is the hardest for you to accept? Why?

Hebrews 10:7-25. Christ's sacrifice on the cross is why we are forgiven. He died to give us that gift—to reconcile us with our Father. We are forgiven to forgive (see Matthew 6:12; Luke 6:37). Hebrews 10:24 tells us to "spur one another on toward love" (NIV). What does that mean to you? How does being forgiven give us the ability to do this? Do you think you will feel free if God forgives you but you don't forgive others? Will it be worth the hard work to get to that point in your life? Even if forgiving costs you something? Remember what our forgiveness cost the Lord. Then maybe it will seem a lot easier.

EXTRA GEM

Ellen White wrote about compassion and forgiveness. Read what she wrote: "If your brethren err, you are to forgive them. When they come to you with confession, you should not say, I do not think they are humble enough. I do not think they feel their confession. What right have you to judge them, as if you could read the heart? The word of God says, 'If he repent, forgive him. And if he trespasses against thee seven times in a day, and seven times in a day turn again to thee, saying, I repent; thou shalt forgive him.' Luke 17:3, 4. And not only seven times, but seventy times seven—just as often as God forgives you" (*Christ's Object Lessons,* p. 249).

Sharing Time

Seventy times seven. That's a big number. And by the time you reach into the 300s or 400s, you're probably getting tired of forgiving. What happens when you reach 491? Will you still forgive?

How can you plan on forgiving? Knowing how you will handle a situation sometimes helps to make it easier. Think: *What can I do to show forgiveness to others who test my patience?* Will you close your eyes and breathe deeply before you open your mouth? Will you pray? Make a list of ideas that can help you when you really need it. Then practice them.

Consider This

Are there things that you haven't let go of—things that others have done to you that you just haven't forgiven? Write them down on paper. Now pray over these. Give them to God. Then rip the paper into tiny pieces and throw them away. Don't go deep-sea diving and try to get them back. Free yourself from the burden of carrying them and let God do it for you. Flying free feels pretty good!

Grace

salvation and Christianity versus legality

This is a perfect chance to lead your young people to the Savior. Pray over this study before giving it. Pray for your young people's hearts!

Icebreaker

Close your eyes and think. It's hot outside. You want a refreshing way to cool down. What pops into your mind? A quick swim or a cool shower? Air-conditioning? How about an old standard used throughout the world—ice cream? We all may scream for ice cream at one time or another. But it's a sure bet that not many will scream for the most expensive sundae on the planet. It's sold in New York City at the whopping price tag of $1,000! It is appropriately named the Grand Opulence Sundae. Its famous garnish is made from 23-karat edible gold. Most people assume only the rich and famous eat these on rare occasions, but the company admits that they sell at least one of these a month. Puts a whole new spin on sweet treats, huh?

So maybe your second choice will be something equally refreshing. With your eyes closed again, can you picture a sweet, mouthwatering, juicy, ruby-red watermelon? Sounds good, huh? The American version is even grown in a seedless form. No more old-fashioned seed-spitting contests! There is nothing like an ice-cold melon on a hot summer day. Out of season, the price tag on these juicy orbs can be expensive. But on the northern island of Hokkaido, Japan, they grow one of the rarest types of watermelon in the world. It is called the Densuke watermelon, and is prized because it is sweeter and firmer than the American variety. The Japanese people purchase these as gifts because they are that good. They are so rare, often only 60 are produced in a season. The most expensive one of these fruits sold at auction for $6,100. Care for a slice?

So the question is Who can afford these luxuries? Perhaps people such as the late Susan Buffett, wife of Warren Buffett, who left $2.5

billion to the foundation they started. This was one of the largest donations ever on record. Then there is Bill and Melinda Gates—the founders of Microsoft—who have given $3 billion.

Dig In

So what do the wealthy do with all their money? Buy ice cream and watermelons? Give it to charity? In the United States, the rich own 41 percent of the nation's wealth.

Yet they donate only 2 percent of their incomes to charity. Being wealthy doesn't mean they've necessarily learned to share the wealth.

But the greatest gift has been given. And it is free. It came at the highest price, too—the death of God's Son. Its name? Grace.

Hot Potato

God's gift of grace allows us to find salvation. Read Ephesians 2:8, 9 and Romans 11:6. Salvation is God's gift. No one can earn it or pay for it. It is far better than the most expensive things in the world. But it remains a gift.

With this gift you can have eternal life. How? Grace allows you to believe that God loves you and wants a personal relationship with you. Looking at His life, it is easy to see that we are all sinners. Admitting that allows His grace to begin working in our lives. But the best part is that knowing Jesus died for us on the cross, we can be sure that He will forgive our sins and give us eternal life. Just ask Jesus into your heart and pray for Him to become your Savior. If you do this, then you've accepted His gift of grace. Grace is a gift that feels wonderful.

Hot Potato Questions

- What do you think holds most people back from accepting God's grace? If it is free, how come it seems so hard to accept?
- Is God's grace really free, or do you have to do something after you accept it? Do you think there are strings attached?
- Do we like to add conditions to God's grace? What do you think God thinks about this? Are there some things that are tradition and not part of God's way? What do you think some of these are? What can you do about it?
- Have you accepted Jesus as your personal Savior? Why or

why not? (Leaders, this is a great time to really talk about this and give your youth a chance to commit their lives to Jesus. Remember to do it with grace.)

Bible Discovery

John 3:16. This is a wonderful place to begin the discussion about grace. Why does this verse tell us that God gave His Son? Does grace have something to do with love? What kind of love would give up an only Son? Love is a core principle of God's character. Do you think that God's love is big enough to include you no matter where you are or what you have done? Do you have to accept a gift in order to receive it?

Hebrews 11:4. What did Cain bring as an offering? Was this a thank offering or a sacrificial offering? Did Cain's offering point forward to a Savior? Why was Abel's sacrifice accepted by God? How did Abel come to God? Do we need to come to Christ, as Abel did, and acknowledge our need of a Savior?

Romans 10:8, 9. Why do you think the Bible tells us that we have to confess our faith? What makes saying it out loud more real? Is it hard to admit to your friends that Jesus is your Savior? Why or why not? Do you remember the old song that tells you not to hide your light under a bushel? If you have a light, don't you want it to shine? Witnessing to others helps us to grow. Can that growth hurt at times? Is God big enough to get us through the rough times?

2 Corinthians 5:17-21. How can God make you into a new creature? Do you think the Holy Spirit helps to do this? When you acknowledge Jesus, does He help you think differently? What does it mean to be reconciled? Does sin take you away from God? Why do you think God wants us to be reconciled with Him? Is it out of love? How can you be an ambassador for Christ? What does an ambassador do? Does being an ambassador for Christ mean that He will work in every aspect of your life?

James 1:27. Are religion and faith the same thing? Why or why not? Can someone do something good (works) for the wrong reason? Can the same "works" be done by two different people—one is good and the other not? If you love God, will you do things that fit with His character? Will you do these things out of love or out of duty? Do humans ever make rules for doing things that displease God? Why or why not? Is God's simple definition of pure religion easy to follow for young people today? Why do you think that way?

EXTRA GEM

Read what Ellen White writes about the wonders of God's grace:

"We should never have learned the meaning of this word 'grace' had we not fallen. God loves the sinless angels, who do His service and are obedient to all His commands, but He does not give them grace. These heavenly beings know nought of grace; they have never needed it, for they have never sinned. Grace is an attribute of God shown to undeserving human beings. We ourselves did not seek after it, but it was sent out in search of us. God rejoices to bestow this grace upon all who hunger for it, not because we are worthy, but because we are so utterly unworthy. Our need is the qualification which gives us the assurance that we shall receive this gift" (*In Heavenly Places*, p. 34).

Sharing Time

Do you have a better understanding of grace and God's gift to you? Why keep it to yourself? Think of one of your friends that needs to hear the truth and freedom that come by God's grace. Pray for that person. Then, go to them and share the story of the greatest gift. Invite them to share in it with you. There is nothing like sharing a gift to make it even more special!

Consider This

Write down the top 10 things you need God to forgive you for. Next, pray about each one of these items. Ask God for forgiveness. Now, here comes the hard part—give these things to God. He will forgive you completely. To remind you of this, tear the paper into tiny pieces and throw it (or burn it) away. It is gone before you know it. Now smile and know that you are free!

Healthy Lifestyle
clean and unclean meats

Leaders, you can't stress enough how fearfully and wonderfully we are made. With young people today, pushing them to choose "healthy" doesn't work as well as explaining how our systems work and guiding them to choose to want to be their best. Often this is done in baby steps, but those are steps forward and closer to God.

Icebreaker

It would be easy to spend your entire life studying about life! Our bodies are the most amazing and complex structures created. God designed them that way, and it can be fun learning about this complex machine.

For instance, how do you feel about walking? Do you like to spend an afternoon or two hiking? Somebody has taken the time to add all those "average" steps up—you know, the ones you take every day—and they've come up with an estimate of how far a person walks in a lifetime. The average person—in their lifetime—walks the equivalent of twice around the world! How does the human body hold up under all those steps? It's amazing!

Sometimes things don't go right with the human body—things that are relatively simple. You've probably experienced this at one time or another. You're minding your own business when your diaphragm involuntarily contracts, causing you to take a quick breath of air into your lungs. The sudden rush of air into the lungs causes the glottis to close, creating a hiccup.

Scientists aren't sure what causes hiccups or how to solve them. There are as many theories as there are proposed cures. They do know that babies in the womb get hiccups. It is thought that the fetus strengthens its diaphragm muscles in preparation for breathing, so that at birth the baby can let out that lusty scream when they see the light of day for the first time. Even pets get hiccups.

Have you ever heard of Charles Osborne? He holds the title of the longest series of hiccups ever recorded—68 years of them! He was a pig farmer, and while working one day in 1922, he got his first hiccup, which continued until things mysteriously stopped one day in May 1990. During that 68-year span,

Osborne married twice, had eight children, and appeared on several television shows. He hiccupped up to 40 times a minute, and scientists estimate that he hiccupped 430 million times in his lifetime. Obviously none of the things he tried, such as closing his eyes and lightly pushing against his eyelids; blowing up a balloon; anticipating the hiccup and saying "beep" right before it; or filling a small paper cup with water, putting his thumbs in his ears, and picking the cup up with his pinkies to drink the water, helped. Sadly, he died one year after the hiccups stopped.

Dig In

We all have experienced hiccups in our lifetime. But these don't involve the diaphragm. Sometimes we learn things that we need to know, but aren't sure how to fit them into our lifestyles. Or maybe we do manage to use them, but don't understand how to tell others about them.

Sometimes that happens when we study God's Word. We understand it and believe it, but it may be difficult to explain to others, or maybe we don't know how to respond to objections. One of these biblical topics is about the use of clean and unclean meats. The Bible is pretty specific about what God's plan is for us and why. But, as always, humans have found a way to find what they are looking for by twisting Scripture, making it possible to live the lifestyle of their choice. People often study the Bible for just that purpose—not for the truth, but to support their own ideas.

Hot Potato

You've all heard the argument—the laws in the Old Testament aren't valid for today. We have all kinds of excuses. But there is no doubt that God had a plan from the beginning. Genesis 1:29 tells us what God wanted us to eat. And it doesn't mention meat. A while later, when humanity had messed up so badly that God had to start over again, a man named Noah was told to build an ark and take in the animals to save them from extinction. Genesis 7:1-3 speaks of the instructions he was given. Notice this happened long before Abraham's children fled from Egypt and were given a godly lecture from Sinai. So the idea that the law was just for the Jews isn't valid.

Hot Potato Questions

- Why do you think people try to find a way around God's laws for our diet? Have you ever had trouble explaining your beliefs to someone else?

- Why do you think eating forbidden meats is so appetizing? Why do you think God told us not to eat them in the first place? Was it because He could, or do you think He had a plan in mind?
- What could that plan be? Is the God of the Old Testament the same God of the New Testament?

Bible Discovery

Matthew 15:11. A lot of people like to use this verse to say they can eat anything. But you need to read the whole chapter to understand this verse. Don't take it out of context by isolating it. Go back and read through verse 20. (Leaders, have someone read Matthew 15:1-20 out loud.) Whom was Jesus talking with in this passage? What were they discussing? What had they accused the disciples of doing? What did Jesus say needed to be clean? Is this passage referring to eating meat? Why or why not? Notice verse 20—Jesus sums it up Himself.

1 Timothy 4:1-5. This is another passage that people like to take out of context. When does this passage say that false teachers will forbid the things listed? Have there already been false teachers in these end days? Do they tell their followers to follow God's law or do they often make up their own interpretation of it? Were unclean meats ever God's intention for people to eat? Were those meats ever considered "good"? The Greek word used here *(Broma)* for "meat" in some translations is actually better interpreted as "food," as you see here in the NIV. Do you think this verse gives permission for people to eat whatever they want as long as they are thankful? Why or why not?

Acts 10. Perhaps this is the most often used passage to explain God's laws. It definitely requires careful study of the entire passage. At the time that Peter was sitting on the roof of the tanner's house, what do you think his attitude was toward the Gentiles (see verse 28)? Do you think God used Peter's hunger to help him understand better? Does God often use natural things to teach us about His Word? Didn't Peter spend three and a half years with Jesus? If the dietary laws were no longer valid, wouldn't Peter know and would he have told God that he had never eaten anything unclean? What does Peter say is the meaning of the vision? Did this vision have anything to do with the eating of unclean meats? Why or why not?

Romans 14. This is one of the last passages most people use to try to prove God's laws are invalid. What two groups are involved in the dispute here? (Leaders, help youth to see that it is a dispute between the Gentile Christians and the Jewish Christians.) In verse 13 Paul lays out the meaning of this passage. What is it? Judging started with Cain and Abel and has continued since—dividing whole churches. The Gentile Christians were mad because the Jewish Christians were buying from the market reduced-priced meat that had been sacrificed to idols. Why do you think this bothered the Gentile Christians? (Leaders, help your youth to see that the Gentiles had previously sacrificed the meat to idols before their conversion, so this was especially difficult for them to accept. The Jewish converts had sacrificed only to the true God, so they didn't have a past association with this practice [see 1 Corinthians 8:4-9].) Do you think Paul was trying to say that unclean meats were now acceptable, or do you think he was trying to help heal the hurt that was present in the church? Would you not do something that you felt was right if it would help a fellow brother or sister?

EXTRA GEM

Ellen White saw that humanity would find a way to reinterpret God's laws. Read what she wrote:

"Among professed Christians today there are many who would decide that Daniel was too particular, and would pronounce him narrow and bigoted. They regard the matter of eating and drinking as of too little consequence to require such a decided choice, one involving the probable sacrifice of every earthly advantage. But in the day of judgment those who reason thus will find that they turned from God's express requirements, and set up their own opinion as a standard of right and wrong. They will find that what seemed to them unimportant was not so regarded by God. His requirements should be sacredly obeyed. Those who accept and obey one of His precepts because it is convenient to do so, while they reject another because its observance would require a sacrifice, lower the standard of right, and by their example lead others to regard lightly His holy law. A 'Thus saith the Lord' is to be our rule in all things" (*Youth's Instructor*, June 4, 1903).

Sharing Time

Help your friends understand the Bible's logic. If the unclean meats were declared unclean before the Flood, when could they have become "clean"? Armed with this logic, you'll be able to help your friends better understand their heavenly Father, who loves them very much!

Consider This

This week, take time to mark the passages you have studied on this subject with notes that will help you as you explain the beauty and consistency of God's laws for our health. Then you'll be armed and ready to help others see the truth about our dietary choices.

Heaven and Hell
choices for eternity

Heaven and hell are very real, and this lesson's aim is to help youth see and understand that, and also to show they have a choice as to where they will spend eternity. Encourage them to dream about heaven and the promise of eternal life!

Icebreaker

It drove one woman to curiosity—the verse in Malachi 3:3. It talks about God's character and says that He "will sit as a refiner and purifier of silver." It was something that the people of biblical times understood, but it isn't something people in our day know much about. So, curious, she found a silversmith and asked if she could come and watch him work through this process.

The silversmith held a piece of silver over a flame to let it heat up. As he worked, he explained what he was doing. He told her how, when working with precious silver, one must hold the piece in the middle of the flame, where the fire is hottest. It was the only way to burn away impurities that would make the silver less valuable.

The woman thought again about the verse in Malachi. She pictured God sitting and having to hold us in the hottest flame to purify us and make us into the people He longed for us to be.

The silversmith explained further that he had to sit and hold the precious piece in the flames the entire time. He had to watch it carefully. If left for even a moment too long, the costly piece could be ruined.

Again, the image of God came to the woman. She pictured God watching carefully over us—His precious creation—not letting anyone perish in the flames. Then another question came to mind.

"How do you know when the silver is refined?" she asked.

The answer was easy. "When I see my image in the silver, it's done," the silversmith replied with a smile.

God is working on you to refine and purify you. Sometimes you may feel the heat. Don't worry. God will not leave you in the flame too long. He is looking for His image in you!

Dig In

Do you ever feel like you are in the middle of the flame? Do you ever get discouraged in your walk with God? Do you ever just get tired and wonder if it is all worth it?

Sometimes our life here on earth is discouraging. It is something everyone experiences at one time or another. Life just gets difficult—so many things to balance! With school, friends, family, church, etc., it is easy to get overwhelmed. So much to do and so little time to do it. You can look forward to a time when things won't be this way—a time when there will be no more deadlines, schoolwork, pain; all those things that hinder, frighten, and hurt will be destroyed in the "twinkling of an eye."

Hot Potato

What some people teach about heaven is astonishing. They are convinced that when we die, if we are right with God, we will immediately go to heaven. The devil is the first one to teach that in the Garden of Eden (see Genesis 3:4). He wanted Adam and Eve and the whole world to come to think that we have an immortal soul—one that can be separated from our body. That's not what God said and not what the Bible teaches.

David understood this. You could show the biblical truth on the soul and the state of the dead just in Psalms! In Psalm 13:3 David calls death a sleep. He understood and taught that we don't go to heaven when we die. He knew that we would sleep until Christ's second coming, and that then, alive or dead, we would be reunited with God and given the glorious gift of heaven!

Hot Potato Questions

- Why do you think so many believe that when a person dies, they go straight to heaven? Would that be a comforting thought or not? Explain why you believe this.
- Does this belief in the immortal soul make sense when God says He will resurrect all His people when He comes?
- Does the promise of heaven make it easier or harder to live on this earth? Why do you feel that way?
- How can we explain the near-death experiences that some talk about in light of the truth about the state of the dead? (Leaders, be prepared to help guide the youth with this issue. Youth are

especially vulnerable to this mistaken belief and easily swayed about these much-talked-about experiences.)

- Do you believe that heaven is a real place? What do you think it will be like there?
- What aspects of heaven do you look forward to the most?
- Do you believe that hell will be real, too?
- What choices can you make to choose where you will spend eternity?

Bible Discovery

1 Thessalonians 4:13-18. What a comforting promise found in these verses. What did Jesus conquer when He rose from the grave? Does that give us hope that even though we die, we can be raised again when Jesus comes? Why is it consistent with God's character to know that the Bible teaches death as a sleep? What are some of the questions you want to ask Jesus when you meet Him face to face?

Matthew 22:23-33. Who were the Sadducees? Did they believe in the resurrection of the dead? What did Jesus want them to know about? Why did He say that He was the God of Abraham, Isaac, and Jacob? Do you think that He wanted them to know that they were safe in His memory and that someday they would live again? Do you think He wants us to know that we will recognize others even after death, that our individual traits and character will still be there, just in a perfect state? (See also Romans 14:8, 9.)

Matthew 25:31-46. The people didn't always understand Jesus. When He said these verses, they thought He was talking about only Himself. They didn't see that how we treat each other is how God will treat us in the end. Do you think it is important to be kind to others, even those who may rub you the wrong way? In heaven, will we be able to get along with everyone? Why then and not now? Should we be practicing? If we aren't right with God, what will be our eternal existence? Is God a God of faithfulness? Can He be trusted to decide our eternity? While we can't earn our way to heaven, can we earn our way to hell? Why or why not? Is hell just as real as heaven to you?

Revelation 21:3-5. We see here one of the best aspects of heaven. God will live with us and we will live with Him. What do you think it will be like when you see God face to face? Is it even possible for us to imagine it? Heaven will be beyond our wildest dreams. The best things here will not even be wonderful any longer because God will create all things new, and you can trust that they will be unimaginable. Do you think that God wants all His children to be there with Him? Since Jesus died for all, what could keep someone from being in heaven? Why might they not want eternal life with God? Can we trust that God will punish those who don't believe in a way that will be right? Does His character prove that out?

Revelation 21:22-27. These are some of the last verses in our Bibles. What a promise! Can you imagine a place without the need for the sun to light it up? The Son will be the light? Unbelievable. Heaven is a real place. If we allow Jesus to be our Lord it is the promise we will receive, not because we deserve it, but because Jesus paid for our ticket there! Why do you think some choose not to be a part of God's kingdom? Does heaven begin for us on this earth? Why do you think this way? If earth can bring us a foretaste of heaven, do you think those who reject God also have a foretaste of hell? Does that explain some of their behavior? Is a person not right with Christ always looking for something to satisfy? Does living for Jesus bring satisfaction and peace? Will God keep His promises and allow us to be a part of His incredible kingdom?

EXTRA GEM

Ellen White was shown how this world is a battlefield now for good and evil and that the promise of heaven to come was a sure thing. Read what she wrote:

"The fallen world is the battlefield for the greatest conflict the heavenly universe and earthly powers have ever witnessed. It was appointed as the theater on which would be fought out the grand struggle between good and evil, between heaven and hell. Every human being acts a part in this conflict. No one can stand on neutral ground. Men must either accept or reject the world's Redeemer. All are witnesses, either for or against Christ. Christ calls upon those who stand under His banner to engage in the conflict with Him as faithful soldiers, that they may inherit the crown of life. They have been adopted as sons and daughters of God. Christ has left them His assured promise that great will be the reward in the kingdom of heaven of those who partake of His humiliation and suffering for the truth's sake" (*Sons and Daughters of God,* p. 242).

Sharing Time

Many people mistake hell as a fire burning forever and ever. Does that fit in with God's character? Read the following texts and see if you can understand what it will mean for those who have not chosen Christ. Jeremiah 31:3 tells us about God's character. Second Peter 3:9 tells us that God doesn't want anyone to miss out on heaven. Malachi 4:1-3 shows us that the unrighteous will be turned to ashes. Ashes are what is left when something is completely consumed, not still burning. In Matthew 25:46 Jesus says that those who reject God will have eternal punishment, not continual punishment. Just as a judge gives a sentence after a court verdict, God will do the same for those who do not choose to follow Him. They have a sentence of death, and once dead, it is over forever. God's character is consistent, and we have to keep that in mind. Study this out, and you will be prepared to help others learn about God's righteous character.

Consider This

What do you think heaven will be like? Do you like to do certain things on this earth, such as bird-watching? Think about all life throughout God's kingdom. Can you see all the birds on this planet in your lifetime? How long would it take you to observe all of them throughout the kingdom of God? Do you think you'll get bored in eternity? Birds not your thing? What is? God wants us to think about heaven and meditate on His character. As you do, you'll see that the promise He has given of eternal life is going to be out of this world!

How to Study the Bible
the written connection with God

Read through the lesson and be prepared for any questions your group may have. What a great opportunity to get your group excited about studying God's Word for themselves!

Icebreaker

Since you've chosen to study the Bible, you'll learn best if you use your preferred learning style. There are three commonly accepted categories into which learners often fit. 1. Auditory learners. If this is you, you probably learn best when things are discussed out loud. You might benefit from listening to audiotapes or reading the material out loud. You really enjoy discussions with others. 2. You might be a tactile or kinesthetic learner if you like the hands-on approach. You like to get physical with your learning. You do best when you can move about and handle things. So you might want to move about as you read and study—have something to write with, hold a pen in your hand to underline important things. 3. Visual learners like the written word. They also like pictures and handouts.

If this is you, keep a special notebook for all the written notes you like to write. Create pictures in your mind as you are reading the material to help you remember.

No one uses one of the styles exclusively. When you were a child you were a kinesthetic learner. All kids are. But as you mature, sometimes that style changes, and it can change with the activities you are doing.

Other factors that affect learning styles include deductive/inductive reasoning. If you like to look at the big picture first, and then get the details, you are a deductive reasoner. You like to know all the rules before you play a game. If you like to learn as you go and see examples of something before you get an overview, then you are an inductive reasoner.

Then there's something called personal versus interpersonal learning. Do you like to figure out things on your own? Do you like doing your homework by yourself instead of with a big group? Then you are probably a personal learner. If making decisions involves advice from family or friends, and you prefer working out problems in a group, then you are an interpersonal learner.

Why is it important to understand your learning style? Because you are about to embark on a great adventure: studying God's Word. And if you know how you learn best, you will get the most out of the fascinating material you are about to discover. You are about to find information that has the power to transform your life! So figure out what's the best way for you to study and dig in. Get ready for a wonderful new time in your life!

Dig In

Is the Bible more than something that gathers dust on a bookshelf? Do you think you would benefit if you spent more time reading your Bible? Why or why not? Reading may be hard for you, so why choose the Bible?

In the dark days before the Reformation, people were not encouraged to read the Bible for themselves. They listened to what their local pastor said about it. Of course, there weren't any printed versions available for home use, and there weren't public libraries to visit. Many people couldn't read, so they trusted someone else to do their reading for them. The period was called the Dark Ages for a reason. People were often in the dark about God.

Today, when others put all their trust in someone else to tell them what the Bible says, often the same results happen. Look at Waco and the Jim Jones cult mass suicide. (Leaders, you may have to present a little about each of these groups to the youth. The point here is to show that when you let others make your choices, sometimes the results can be disastrous!) They depended on their leaders to interpret God's Word, and the leaders failed their groups miserably by twisting it into something that brought death instead of life.

Hot Potato

Did you know that several of the early editions of the Bible translated into English contained infamous mistakes? In 1560 the Geneva Bible was nicknamed the "Breeches Bible" because Genesis 3:7 read, "They sewed fig leaves together and made themselves breeches." In 1631 the Wicked Bible dropped the word "not" from an important verse. Look it up, Exodus 20:14, and you'll see why it got its nickname. In 1702 the King James Bible contained a flaw in Psalm 119:161. It erroneously read: "Printers have persecuted me without cause."

Hot Potato Questions
- The Bible contains 66 books written by more than 40 authors, and

it was written over a 1,500-year period of time. So how can you know if the Bible is true to its word?

- What makes studying it worth your investment of time?
- Why study it for yourself? Why not just let others tell you about it?

Bible Discovery

Psalm 119:160. King David had a living relationship with God. He knew Scripture and had something to say about it. If David trusted God's Word, do you think you can?

2 Timothy 3:16. Paul wrote to Timothy. Remember him? Paul was the one persecuting Christians until God hit him with His light. Look up what Paul says about Scripture. Do you think that he is correct? Do you trust that all Scripture is "God-breathed"? How is that possible? Do you think it could have something to do with the work of the Holy Spirit?

Romans 15:4. Do you want to find hope and encouragement? Need guidance? Paul tells us a way of finding it in God's Word. Check it out!

John 5:39. Do you think that studying will help you understand God more? Check out what Jesus said about the Scriptures.

Psalm 119:9-12. Back to King David—he was a pretty cool dude with a great relationship with God. He had sons and daughters that he wanted to tell about God. And he wanted them to learn. What did he say about living and learning? Read this section and see. (The only way to put something into your heart is to see it first. So, you have to read God's Word to store it in your heart.)

When you study, don't forget to start with prayer. God will be more able to open your heart and hide His Word in it. And don't forget to ask for the help of the Holy Spirit. Jesus tells us to do this in John 14:26. Check it out. You may also want to have a highlighter and pen ready to make notes about what you are learning.

EXTRA GEM

Ellen White loved to read God's Word, too! And God showed her that in the Scriptures we would find God's true character: Check out this quote from one of her books, *Thoughts From the Mount of Blessing,* page 26:

"The pure in heart discern the Creator in the works of His mighty hand, in the things of beauty that comprise the universe. In His written word they read in clearer lines the revelation of His mercy, His goodness, and His grace. The truths that are hidden from the wise and prudent are revealed to babes. The beauty and preciousness of truth, which are undiscerned by the worldly-wise, are constantly unfolding to those who have a trusting, childlike desire to know and to do the will of God."

Sharing Time

Now that you've discovered some important truths about God's Word, why keep them to yourself? Can you think of some ways that you might share Scripture with others this week? How about writing your favorite verses on a note card and memorizing them? As others see you do this, they may ask you what you are doing. And what good news you will have to share with them. Can you think of other ways?

Second Timothy 2:15 tells us, "Do your best to present yourself to God as one approved, a worker who does not need to be ashamed and who correctly handles the word of truth" (NIV).

Consider This

Write out one thing you can do this week that will help you find time to study God's Word more for yourself.

Humility

small but mighty in God's sight

Humility means relying on God's strength and not yours. Remember, God created each person with their own unique personality. Being comfortable with who you are frees you to care about others. Help your young people understand that God loves them as they are and wants to change their hearts so that others are important to their mission.

Icebreaker

At birth her name was Agnes Gonxha Bojaxhiu, but we don't know her by that. She wasn't very tall or very rich. Yet she was awarded a Nobel Prize. People all over the world know of her work, and it doesn't matter what your faith is, she set an example for all to follow.

We know her as Mother Teresa, and she had one goal since she was 12 years old: to serve humanity and spread the love of Jesus. And she did just that for more than 40 years, helping some of the poorest people on the earth.

At the time of her death she left a legacy of associates to carry on the work she helped to establish, operating missions in 123 countries. They include homes for people with HIV/AIDS, leprosy, tuberculosis, soup kitchens, children's programming, orphanages and schools, and family counseling centers.

All because one little girl determined in her heart that God was big enough to do big things, and that He would choose to use her if she was willing. She served Him willingly and humbly until her death. Did she do everything perfectly? No. But she didn't let that stop her. Did she let the fame she received go to her head? No. She remained humble all of her days.

Dig In

Do you think God can use you the same way He used Mother Teresa? Just like Agnes—who was born poor and died poor—God starts with a willing heart. But how easy is it to be humble in this world in which greed and pride seem to be the norm?

Do you look at others and want to be like them? Who are those others? Stars, sports heroes, musicians? Are these the people you look to as your example of greatness? What kind of spirit do they portray? Are they humble and grateful for what they have been given, or do they flaunt their fame for everyone to see?

So why should you want to be humble?

Is it something God really wants for you?

Hot Potato

Most people think that what the Bible teaches about humility makes you a wimp. So is that what God really wants for you, to be a wimp? Jesus is the perfect example of a humble life. Do you think He was a wimp? Read again where Jesus threw the money changers and sellers out of the Temple (John 2:12-23). Close your eyes and picture it. Do you see Jesus asking them politely to get moving?

While your eyes are closed, picture Jesus again. He is 30 years old and working as a carpenter. Do you think He was stick thin and lacking muscles? Humility doesn't require a lack of strength. Humility relies on God's strength, something Jesus understood and practiced. It doesn't mean groveling, either. When you are humble in the Lord, He will make you strong. It doesn't mean putting on a false front, because the more you know God, the less you have to prove. It doesn't mean cowering, because you can talk lovingly in any situation, even if it involves being firm or taking action. Being humble gets results—most often more than being brash and bold. It means not having to always win but still being happy.

Hot Potato Questions

- How do you define humility? (Leaders, take the time to talk this one out and write down all the answers. One aspect often forgotten is that humility is about being comfortable with who you are in the Lord, and that makes you free to put others first.)
- How do verses such as Matthew 11:29 fit in with that description? Is serving others humility?
- Can you still think that you are a good person and be humble? Why or why not?
- Does the Bible point to the fact that true humility is loving others? Can you do that and still be yourself?
- Do you have to deny your strengths and gifts to be truly humble? Why or why not?

Bible Discovery

Jeremiah 17:9. One of the first steps in looking at humility is to examine your motives. Why are you taking the action that you are? Is what I am doing honoring God or making me look better? Pride is a tricky thing. We should have pride in what God has done for us, but there is a line that can be crossed. What should our motive be in anything we do?

Proverbs 8:13. Does God like pride? How much do you think He hates it? Why would God have a problem with us having too much pride? (Leaders, remember the origin of sin.) How can you have good pride in something? What can be the result of too much pride? Is it easy to do good things and not have some pride? Why do you think that is?

James 4:10; Proverbs 8:13. Why do you think God tells us to humble ourselves before Him? How can you do that? Is God looking for false humility or a humble heart? Do you think God wants you to act a certain way or live a certain way? Is there a difference? Why or why not? How does it make you feel when someone else gives you an unsolicited compliment? Do you think that is what God means when He says "He will lift you up" (NIV)? Why is it better to let someone else sing your praises rather than pointing out the good that you do yourself?

Philippians 2:3. How can we consider others better than ourselves? Does this mean in our actions or just our thoughts? What are some of the ways that you can do things for others? Do they have to be big things, or can they be simple things? Can small things have a big impact? Do you think some people do things for others to get attention or for selfish ambition? Why would they do that? Do you think that humility is an action word?

Philippians 2:5-8. How can we have the same attitude as Jesus? Did He gain strength in prayer? What ways can you (as an individual and as a group) do as Jesus did? Make a list of things that you can accomplish to serve others and pray over this list. Choose at least one thing and set a goal as to how you can and will accomplish this. Will it be easy for you to have the same attitude that Jesus did? Why or why not? Do things around us influence us to be proud and boastful? Is it in our nature to be servants? What is the best way for us to have the heart of a servant? What will the reward of a servant be? Is this possible because Jesus became our servant and gave His life for us?

EXTRA GEM

Ellen White encourages us with the following words about humility:

"From the root of true humility springs the most precious greatness of mind, greatness which leads men to conform to the image of Christ. Those who possess this greatness gain patience and trust in God. Their faith is invincible. Their true consecration and devotion keep self hidden. The words that fall from their lips are molded into expressions of Christlike tenderness and love. Having a sense of their own weakness, they appreciate the help which the Lord gives them, and they crave His grace that they may do that which is right and true. By their manner, their attitude, and their spirit, they carry with them the credentials of learners in the school of Christ" (*Review and Herald*, May 11, 1897).

Sharing Time

Read Matthew 5:5. In this verse, the words Jesus uses can be translated from the Greek to mean: "A wild stallion under the control of God." Does that change the way you think of humility? A stallion is still a stallion, but under God's control, it has submitted itself to the "bit"—the steel placed in the horse's mouth to control it. It has made a choice. Others may think that you are weak if you are a Christian. Armed with the knowledge you have now, can you show your friends that being a Christian and being humble are not signs of weakness but of strength? Be bold for God this week. Find a way to help someone else in a way that you haven't before. Then when they ask, tell them it is because you love Jesus and are His servant. When they ask you what that means, be ready to answer.

Consider This

Make a list of ways you would like to be able to help others. Look at your talents, prioritize the list, and make plans to carry out the first item on it. Just don't stop there! Be brave! You have God's strength to rely on.

Loneliness

loneliness in the church

Many adults think that they are the only ones who experience loneliness. This is not true. Young people can feel a profound sense of loneliness. It fuels many of the behaviors that can be destructive in their lives. Be sensitive to this need. Sometimes the ones that you think are the least susceptible to this are the loneliest of all.

Icebreaker

Most people love them, but for some, the sight of white-faced, baggy-dressed, big-red-nosed clowns inspire terror. That's not their purpose, though. Clowns are meant to entertain and to bring laughter, especially to young children.

The history of clowns goes back thousands of years. The first clowns were court jesters and the only ones allowed to speak out against the ruler's ideas. They were allowed to use their humor to change royal policy. And some of the bravest clowns did just that.

Yu Sze was one such clown. He was the royal jester for the Chinese emperor Shih Huang-ti. Shih Huang-ti oversaw the building of the Great Wall of China. During its construction thousands of laborers were killed. Shih Huang-ti wanted to take the wall one step further, and it was his idea to paint the entire thing! Although many knew this would cause more deaths, no one was brave enough to speak up against the emperor's plans. No one except Yu Sze. Doing what he did best, he jokingly convinced the emperor to abandon his plans and leave the Great Wall unpainted, saving thousands of his fellow citizens in the process. Yu Sze is still remembered today as a great Chinese national hero.

Auguste clowns—those with the sloppy clothing, big shoes, large noses, and lots of makeup—are perhaps the most widely known clowns today. The first was an American acrobat named Tom Belling. While performing in Germany with his circus group in 1869, he was punished for not performing his tricks well and neglecting to show discipline. His punishment? He was confined to his dressing room. Out of boredom, he put on some baggy clothing and began imitating the show manager for his friends. When the manager stepped into the room to watch Belling's antics, Tom ran out and ended up in the arena. There, he tripped over the ring, fell flat on his face, and made the audience laugh out loud. From then on, Belling was ordered to keep up this new character, and a whole new world of clowning began.

Dig In

Besides laughing with the clowns, what does this have to do with you? Some people say that clowns hide their sadness behind the mask of their makeup. By assuming a different personality, they can hide the sorrow and the loneliness they feel in their hearts.

Have you ever felt that way? Have you put on a mask of happiness for your friends and family while feeling something far different deep inside your heart? If you have, you are not alone. Almost one third of people admit that they feel lonely. That goes for people of all ages—not just the elderly—but young people as well.

At a time in your life when everything is changing and you are expected to keep up, finding someone you trust with your feelings may seem difficult. It is easy to think that others are not experiencing what you are, and so you might have a tendency to keep your feelings hidden inside where friends and family can't see them. You put on a mask of outward happiness, but inside, you feel anything but happy.

Hot Potato

Maybe you've forgotten—or maybe you never knew—but you are passionately loved! Yes, you! Your heavenly Father thinks you are terrific! He created you and knows you, and yes, despite all your flaws He loves you with an indescribable love.

We all want that kind of love—a love that is unchanging and something we will never get tired of. If you looked all over the world, you'd never find someone who can meet all your needs or your desires. That person does not exist. That's because God created you with a desire to find that kind of love, and it can be found only in Him. You can search all you want, but you'll never find what you are missing until you claim Jesus as Lord of your life.

But that doesn't stop us from looking, does it? Young people are especially vulnerable to trying to fill this void. They often turn to things that destroy their lives, not build them up, such as drugs, alcohol, and sex. Others say that these things will help you find what you are missing, but the truth is they will leave you with more pain than you started with. But even if you are wiser and unwilling to let these things destroy your life, you may still feel lonely.

Hot Potato Questions

- Why do you think so many young people feel lonely even if they go to church? Why doesn't fellowship within the church satisfy one's loneliness?
- Is it possible to be popular and still feel lonely? Why or why not?
- Do you think everyone in your church feels that they belong? Do we ever dehumanize people? Do we forget what it is like to walk in their shoes?
- Do we have expectations of others that we don't hold ourselves to? Could that make us angry or lonely?
- Do you ever keep your loneliness a secret because you don't think Christians should feel that way? Should they? Why or why not?
- Did the prophets of God ever feel this type of loneliness? What can we learn from this?

Bible Discovery

Isaiah 41:10. Is it easy to be fearful when we are lonely? Have you ever felt this way? In this verse what does God say He will do? If we lean on God, can we be sure that He will not let us down the way others may? Can having a personal relationship with God ease the loneliness we may be feeling? Why or why not?

Romans 8:35-39. Does Paul say that there is anything that can keep us from the love of God? Do you believe this promise? Is there anything Paul left out that can keep us from the love of God? Can we do anything to take ourselves away from God? Why or why not?

Habakkuk 3:17-19. Are these verses from the Old Testament an echo of what Paul was saying in the New Testament? Habakkuk was different from some of the other prophets in the Old Testament. Instead of telling what the Lord said, he asked God questions. And the Lord answered him. Things around him were falling apart—especially religious reform. Yet he didn't give up and knew that God wouldn't either. Can we learn to have this kind of trust in our God during the storms we face? Can being lonely feel like a storm? Do you think God understands this?

Psalm 34 (especially verse 18). David wrote this psalm. What did he say in verse 18 that we can take to heart today? David had fled to Gath to escape Saul and thought he had found a place of refuge. But he was recognized and his life was in danger. He pretended to be insane to escape Abimelech. Do you think David experienced loneliness? How did he handle it when he felt lonely? How can we follow his example?

1 Peter 5:7. Will people let us down? Even our friends? Where can we go when we need strength to help us? Do you believe Jesus is strong enough to handle all your fears? Why or why not? Did Jesus ever feel lonely when He was on the earth? Do you think He understands you, then? If we don't have to carry our cares, will that make us better able to help others who are experiencing loneliness?

EXTRA GEM

Ellen White wrote the following to encourage us:

"The life in which the fear of the Lord is cherished will not be a life of sadness and gloom. It is the absence of Christ that makes the countenance sad, and the life a pilgrimage of sighs. Those who are filled with self-esteem and self-love do not feel the need of a living, personal union with Christ. The heart that has not fallen on the Rock is proud of its wholeness. Men want a dignified religion. They desire to walk in a path wide enough to take in their own attributes. Their self-love, their love of popularity and love of praise, exclude the Savior from their hearts, and without Him there is gloom and sadness. But Christ dwelling in the soul is a wellspring of joy. For all who receive Him, the very keynote of the word of God is rejoicing" (*Christ's Object Lessons*, p. 162).

Sharing Time

What can you do if you or a friend is experiencing loneliness?
- Pray for guidance in making a new friend. Pray that God will direct you to the right person and that God will help you be the right person. Pray that your paths will cross.
- To make friends, you have to be friendly yourself. Watch your body language. Practice smiling if you need to. Disarm others with your personality—you are a unique person!

- Get outside of your usual comfort zone. Remember that others are wanting friends as much as you are. Make the first step. You will be pleasantly surprised.
- Start or join a group at your church. Look for things that interest you—places where you can use your talents. Find something, and do it, even if you are uncomfortable. It may grow on you!

Consider This

Loneliness is something many experience even inside the church. Maybe you know someone who feels this way. They probably want to reach out to you but don't know how. This week, look around and see if you can find someone who needs a friend. Be the first to reach out to them, even if you are feeling lonely. The first step is often the hardest, but it also brings with it new adventures and friendship. You can be the start of something great this week!

Lying

lying and profanity

Along with this Bible study you might want to talk with your young people about whether it is ever right to lie. Be prepared—this is a hot topic and should lead to a lively discussion.

Icebreaker

It's a story told throughout the world, just with different names. It has many important lessons if you are willing to listen. The one people remember most? His nose, of course!

Pinocchio—the wooden puppet that wanted to be a real boy. It's of course fiction, but how many times does fiction imitate real life?

Pinocchio gets into all kinds of trouble in his quest for real life. But he has someone to help him stay out of trouble—a little cricket. The cricket constantly warns Pinocchio that he is making wrong choices, but Pinocchio doesn't listen.

As Pinocchio continues to follow his own wishes, he forgets about the father that created him. He soon discovers that pleasure and trouble often go hand in hand. But he doesn't stop until he realizes he is living for himself only and that others are being hurt because of it. Then, and only then, does Pinocchio get his wish, and he becomes a real boy.

Dig In

Does anything about Pinocchio's story sound vaguely familiar? It should. Whether Carlo Collodi, the author of *The Adventures of Pinocchio,* meant it or not, there are a lot of parallels to Christianity in this story first published in 1883.

You too have a Father who created you and gave you life. He loves you enough to set you free and even lets you make choices He is not in favor of. He also came to find you and save you. You also have a little "cricket" (a conscience). You know Him as the Holy Spirit, and just as in Pinocchio, he works on your heart and mind and doesn't leave your side to let you wander on your own. The Holy Spirit works time after time to remind you of the truth, but do you always listen? Pinocchio didn't, and it caused many pitfalls that could have been avoided.

Hot Potato

If you don't remember the whole story of Pinocchio, don't worry. Most people don't. What everyone remembers most is the part about his nose. You see, one of Pinocchio's biggest problems was his unwillingness to stop lying. People lie mainly for two reasons: either to get out of/stay out of trouble or pride. People lie to cover their actions, too—actions they shouldn't have taken in the first place. It is easier to explain away the trouble than to face what might happen if we own up. But is it right?

That's where the Holy Spirit comes in. Have you heard that little voice encouraging you not to be afraid? That's His job, and He wants the truth for you so much, He will keep coming back until you finally get the message.

The other reason most people don't tell the truth is because of pride. Pride led to sin in the first place. Pride still leads there today as we desire people's approval more than God's. Pinocchio had a special appendage that should have helped him—his nose. It grew with each lie he told. And by the end of the story—at least in the Disney version—it grew long enough that birds built a nest on the end of it and roosted there! The more we practice lying, the easier it becomes, and the less we can hear the Holy Spirit's guidance.

Lying often begins inside, right at the heart level. And it is not the only problem we encounter involving our mouths and hearts. All you have to do is stop and listen when you are out in the world. You'll hear words that will make you cringe. You can't even watch television anymore without hearing words that used to be banned from the airwaves. And even in the classroom, foul language isn't confined to just students anymore. Public school teachers are catching up with their students in their choice of words and the right to use them.

You know the Bible has a lot to say about lying and foul language. And maybe it isn't a problem with you. That's terrific! But for many, it is. So whether to help yourself or someone you care about, it doesn't hurt to take a look at what the Bible says about lying and profanity, and see if you, like Pinocchio, can live the real life your Father dreams for you.

Hot Potato Questions

- Do you think there are substitute words for swear words that are OK to use? Is it ever OK to tell a lie?

Bible Discovery

John 8:44. Jesus says that the devil is the father of all lies. Whom was He talking to when He said these words? Look back and review the preceding verses. Weren't these the people He came to save? Do you think Jesus wanted them to truly see themselves?

Does Jesus do this for us, to give us a chance to change and grow?

Genesis 3:4, 5. What was Satan's first lie? Did he try to trick Eve into believing that she had immortality? This was the first lie told on the earth. Satan wanted to confuse humanity about the cost of sin, but it is clear in Romans 6:23 that the wages of sin is death. This lie has caused many to look incorrectly at what death is. Lies do that—they grow and grow into something bigger than they started out to be. And it takes all kinds of energy to keep perpetuating them. Is God's way of truth easier to live with? Explain why you think the way you do.

James 1:26. What does God want us to keep in control? Is this easy to do today? Do you think God understands that? Is He patient in wanting to help us bring our hearts and our mouths under control? Why would your religion be worthless if you were known for telling lies and using profanity? If the world knows that these are not things Christians should be practicing, shouldn't we?

James 3:8-12. What do you think James meant when he said that "no man can tame the tongue"? Do you think that he meant in one's own strength? Why does he say that you can't bless and curse with the same mouth? How can you apply this lesson to your life?

Ephesians 4:29. How can our words help to build others up? Can the wrong words tear others down? Is it easier to build up or to tear down? Why do you think this? How long does it take to correct a misplaced word that hurts someone else? To live like this means that we are thinking about others more than ourselves. Do you think that this is what God wants us to do? Is it worth the effort? What are the rewards of practicing control over your words? (Leaders, be prepared with answers for this and encourage your young people to see the positive side of living God's way.)

Numbers 23:19. Does God ever lie? Can He? What does that promise mean to you? God tells us that lying is wrong. Does He also say that He will forgive us if we use words that we shouldn't? Knowing that God keeps His promises should help us have hope that we will be forgiven and that He will help us become the people He longs for us to be. (See also 2 Peter 3:9.)

EXTRA GEM

Ellen White understood about lying and profanity being accepted by society. Read what she wrote in *Thoughts From the Mount of Blessing*, pages 67, 68:

"Jesus proceeded to lay down a principle that would make oath taking needless. He teaches that the exact truth should be the law of speech. 'Let your speech be, Yea, yea; Nay, nay: and whatsoever is more than these is of the evil one.' These words condemn all those meaningless phrases and expletives that border on profanity. They condemn the deceptive compliments, the evasion of truth, the flattering phrases, the exaggerations, the misrepresentations in trade, that are current in society and in the business world. They teach that no one who tries to appear what he is not, or whose words do not convey the real sentiment of his heart, can be called truthful."

Sharing Time

Be bold this week for the Lord. If you hear someone using language they shouldn't be using, don't be afraid to speak up. Be especially aware of when someone is using God's name in a bad way. Stand up for your Father, because He loves to do that for you!

Consider This

Think about the words that you say. Do you use words that are substitutes for swearing? Are these right to use? Pray about it this week and listen for the Holy Spirit's guidance.

Millennium

1,000 years with Christ

Too many adults believe that young people raised in the church understand the doctrines and teachings without question. Spend this time with your group helping them have a new vision of heaven and to see how important the millennium is in God's plan for a world without sin.

Icebreaker

Her name is Jeanne Louise Calment. You probably never knew her, but you may have heard of her. She lived her whole life in Arles, France. Her entire life consisted of 44,724 days. Don't get out a calculator—we'll translate that for you. It comes to 122 years plus 164 days. According to records she was the oldest living person ever. Others have surfaced through the years, but they don't have the records to challenge Jeanne Louise's claim to fame. Of course, the *Guinness World Records* people weren't around when Methuselah walked the earth!

Born in 1875, Jeanne Louise lived with her parents until she married at the age of 21. Jeanne Louise then was able to live a life of luxury. Her husband, a wealthy store owner, made sure that she never had to work. So instead she pursued such hobbies as tennis, cycling, swimming, roller skating, and piano. She outlived her husband, their only daughter, and her grandson. At age 90 she struck a deal to sell her apartment to a then-47-year-old on terms of a reverse mortgage. That meant he would pay her a fixed sum each month until her death. She outlived him, too!

She lived on her own until starting a small fire in her apartment during a cooking accident. By then she was partly blind, and things were becoming more difficult for her to see. But even at the nursing home she continued to move about freely. A fall just one month shy of her 115th birthday forced her to become more sedentary, though she still remained somewhat independent, refusing to ask others for help.

Her real claim to fame came in 1956, when she starred in a movie about famed painter Vincent Van Gogh, whom she had met at the age of 13. At the age of 114 she became the oldest actress ever, again having a role in a movie about Van Gogh. Five months before her death in 1997, she gave up doing any more public performances.

Dig In

It's hard to imagine living 122 years plus 164 days! Can you imagine the changes in our world that she saw during her life? Transportation alone meant she witnessed the change from horse-drawn vehicles to automobiles to air planes and jets to rockets launched into outer space. And technology? Forget about telegraphing news, now you can witness it in real time on your cell phone if you live in Japan! She saw all kinds of wars, democracies, medical advances that would blow the mind at the time of her birth.

It's hard to imagine living that long, but it is something that will happen to all God's children someday soon. In fact, 122 years won't even come close to the records about to be made. Forever can't be measured, or imagined.

Hot Potato

When Jesus comes again—a promise we can believe in—we will live 1,000 years with Him and our heavenly Father in heaven! We call it the millennium, a word to wrap our human minds around. But can we? Those 1,000 years are just the beginning of a life that will no longer be measured in years.

So why the 1,000? What makes this time different from the rest of eternity?

It will be a time of rejoicing in heaven, a time to look at all that God has made for us and to experience His love firsthand. It will also be a time of judgment, during which God in His graciousness lets us look at the book of the lives of our loved ones who aren't there with us, to examine why their choices didn't support their living in heaven, and to let us draw the same conclusion that He has: that they would never be content in heaven and that sin needs to be done away with forever. God's righteousness will reign, and He will let all see that He is not only sovereign but also gracious and fair.

It will also be a time for reflection for the one that brought sin to our world. The devil will roam the earth alone, with no power to exert, because all will be dead. He will live on the earth that his sin cursed in a state of destruction. The plagues will have spoiled the earth for habitation, and everyone not among God's children will have been slain by the very brightness of His coming. (Leaders, help the young people to see that this is the first death.) He will have 1,000 years to think about all he has done to the earth and its people, all that sin caused, all that death created, and the punishment that is to come for him and all those he fooled through the ages.

Hot Potato Questions

- What does it tell you about God's character, that He will give us the chance to help judge those not in heaven?
- Do you think knowing we will spend this time with God in heaven will help us make it through the difficult days just prior to His coming?
- Does eternity make you excited, or does it scare you? Why do you feel that way?
- Do you think God can help us spend this time with Him reviewing the lives of others we love, and help us not to be sad?
- Do you think it is fair that the devil will have these 1,000 years alone to meditate on all that he has done? Why do you think God gives him this time instead of just destroying him?

Bible Discovery

John 14:1-3. When did Jesus give this promise? What was He trying to do for His dis- ciples? Is this a promise only for the disciples, or does it also apply to all who believe? Does Jesus keep His promises? Always? If He says that He will come again in a literal way, can we trust that that will happen? Does this promise bring comfort to you, too?

1 Thessalonians 4:13-18. Jesus will return, and that marks the beginning of the millennium. Who will be the first to meet Him in the air? Why do you think the righteous dead will be called first before those who are still alive? When will those who lived through the very last days get to meet Jesus in the clouds? Do you think there will be any sadness for those who love God on that day? Why or why not?

Revelation 20:1-3. Where will the devil spend the thousand years? Why is the earth described as an abyss? Do you think the plagues will have destroyed things here? Will there be any people for the devil to mislead? What happened to those that were alive but didn't believe in Jesus at the second coming? Is this what the Bible calls the "first death"? (See also Jeremiah 4:23-28.)

Revelation 20:4-6. What do you think it means when the Bible says that we will reign with Christ? Does it mean that we get to take part in the judgment of the wicked? Who gets to take part in the "first resurrection"? Which resurrection is it important to be a part of? Why? Is it our choice to make? What choices can we make in our lives that will help us be a part of the first resurrection?

Revelation 20:7-15. What happens at the end of the 1,000 years? Can we be sure that God will prevail and that Satan can no longer win? How do you know this? Will all be judged for their choices? What is the final punishment for their sins? Do you think separation from God will be a terrible thing to bear? Who will be part of the "second death"? Do you think this time will go on and on, or does the character of God tell us it will have an end? Is this second death a choice? When is that choice made? How can we make sure that we aren't part of this second death?

Revelation 21:1-4. When will the earth be made new? Is it after the millennium? Will God have a residence with us on the earth made new? What other promise do these verses have for us? Do you think we will mourn anymore for those that were lost? Why or why not? Can you even begin to imagine what this earth will look like when it is new from the Creator's hand? Don't you want to explore it? Can you see that things will be so wonderful that you want to be a part of God's everlasting kingdom? What choices do you need to make for your life today?

EXTRA GEM

Ellen White was given a vision of heaven. Read what she wrote:

"Language is altogether too feeble to attempt a description of heaven. As the scene rises before me, I am lost in amazement. Carried away with the surpassing splendor and excellent glory, I lay down the pen, and exclaim, 'Oh, what love! What wondrous love!' The most exalted language fails to describe the glory of heaven or the matchless depths of a Savior's love" (*The Faith I Live By*, p. 352).

Sharing Time

Do your friends believe differently than you do about the millennium? What can you share with them that will help them see where we will spend this time and what we will be doing? Write down the verses that help you understand about the millennium on 3" x 5" cards and memorize them. Then you will be able to lead others in a study about this wonderful event, and maybe help them to understand why making the right choices here will affect where they will spend eternity.

Consider This

Read Ellen White's vision of heaven in *Early Writings,* pages 16-20. It will help you see how unbelievable heaven will be as she tries to relate in words some of the glory she had been shown. Reading it should help you have a new desire for God's kingdom.

My Commitment to the Church

baptism, Communion, evangelism

This study is intended to review the baptismal vows and the young people's commitment to the church and to God. It can be used for those who haven't yet chosen baptism. It is meant to help them understand how being a citizen here is like being a citizen in heaven. We have commitments that we need to fulfill.

Icebreaker

No matter where you live in the world, there are laws that your government has made that you must obey or you will get a ticket, or worse. When most are enacted it is for a clear purpose: to keep the citizens safe. But looking back through the archives, we have to wonder what our forefathers were thinking!

Did you know that it is illegal in Palm Springs, California, to walk a camel down the main street between 4:00 and 6:00 p.m.? No camel walking during rush hour. Now, that's a problem. Speaking of animals, next time you drive in Arcadia, California, watch out for peacocks. They have the right of way on public streets. So if you see one, you have to yield to it. Somebody in California must really like animals!

Want to visit a bed and breakfast? You can in Derby, Kansas, if you screech your tires. And the price is right: you can get up to 30 days free at the Bad Boy's B&B (the local jail). And while we are on cars, be careful if you are in Oregon. Shut your car door as quickly as possible, because otherwise you might just get a ticket for keeping it open too long! Makes you wonder what prompted this one!

If you live in Denmark, watch how you order that all-important glass of water. A law there allows the restaurant to charge you only if they put ice and lemon in your glass. How do you tip for that? And watch how you drive around horses there. If the car you are driving comes upon a horse-drawn carriage and the horse becomes agitated, you must pull over and cover the car so the horse cannot see you. Now, there's some horse sense!

Ever have the urge to do something funny? Like pay your bill in pennies? Well, forget it if you live in Canada. Any debt more than 25 cents cannot be paid in pennies. The beauty is in the details in Toronto where it is against the law to ride a streetcar on Sunday if you've been eating garlic! Yep, you read that right. If you've been around someone eating raw garlic, you'll probably agree. It may be healthy for them but not so much for you!

Dig In

All kidding aside, most laws are made with a benefit in mind. And God's laws are no exception. His laws are made with us in mind—our safety, our happiness, our completeness. But sometimes desiring them in a sinful world is about as easy as yielding to peacocks. Possible but not probable.

Why is it so hard to do what God asks? On the day of our baptism into God's family, we stand before a congregation and agree that the 29 fundamental beliefs of the Seventh-day Adventist Church are something that we have read, studied, and agree to—both in our minds and our hearts. How long is it before that vow has less meaning to us? How long before the world's allure pulls us subtly, or not so subtly, from keeping those vows?

Hot Potato

Making a commitment to God on the day of your baptism is much like making a wedding vow. To God, that vow is sacred. You have become part of His covenant and inherited the promise of that covenant, and it's a promise that He keeps forever. Only His commitment doesn't end with "till death do us part." His promises last way beyond what the grave can do. His promise is eternal life, and He wants to give you that gift. Oh, how He longs to give you that gift. So why the broken promises on our end?

This world is full of sin. So often we make promises rashly. Then we let this thing called life pull us away without giving it a second thought. But shouldn't we give it a second thought? Maybe laws like this one in Michigan have become archaic: it is illegal to hitch a crocodile to a fire hydrant. But the vows that you took at baptism are not only worth honoring; they were taken straight from God's Word. They will never become archaic because God is not archaic, and His laws and His word will be valid throughout eternity.

Hot Potato Questions

- Have you already made the decision and been baptized into God's family? If you haven't, what is keeping you from making this all-important decision? Were you baptized because it was something you desired, or did you feel pressured into doing it?

- Did you understand all the fundamental beliefs? Which ones are the hardest to understand and perhaps implement in your life?
- Do you think you should honor the vows that you have made? Do you think God understands that it may be hard to keep our commitment in a world full of sin?
- Do you think He forgives us when we make mistakes?
- Do you think we should do our best to honor God and not just rely on His forgiveness?
- What can making a habit of relying on forgiveness do to our commitment to God?
- Should we make an effort to change our ways?
- Do you believe God's laws of love are valid and worth putting into practice in your life?

Bible Discovery

Psalm 85:10. What do you think it means that "righteousness and peace kiss each other" (NIV)? Where can you find the best example of love and faithfulness meeting? Is it at Calvary? Looking at Christ's sacrifice for us, is it easier for you to keep the choice you made when you took your baptismal vows? If you haven't been baptized, can understanding God's law as love and faithfulness help you to reach a decision about joining God's family?

Ephesians 4:14-16. Why should we continue to study after we have made our commitment to the church? Does studying bring growth? Can the devil try to trick us into not honoring our commitment if we don't continue to study from God's Word? Why is it easy in this world of sin to get tossed about in respect to our faith?

Ecclesiastes 5:1-5. Why doesn't God want us to make vows unless we intend to keep them? What do you think the Bible means by the "sacrifice of fools" (NIV)? Do you think it means a literal sacrifice? Does this remind you of the story of the publican and the Pharisee? (See Luke 18:9-14.) Which one in that story offered the "sacrifice of fools"? Why do you think God would rather us wait until we mean our vows before we say them? Is making them part of building a relationship with God? Should we wait until we are perfect to begin that relationship and be baptized? Why or why not? Is it possible to keep all your vows to the church? Is it probable? Does God understand?

1 Corinthians 11:23-26. Why do you think participating in Communion is like a miniature baptism? How is this an obligation to God and to the church? Does Communion, especially with the foot-washing service, put us all on level ground? Is this what God wants for us, to help build unity in the church? Can obeying your commitment to the church make you a servant? Is that a good thing or a bad thing? Why do you feel this way? Why do you think Jesus instituted the Last Supper and asked that we follow it until He comes?

1 Peter 3:15, 16. What hope is this verse speaking of? Are you prepared to be able to explain to others the reason for your hope? Why or why not? What do you need to do to be ready? How is this an obligation to God and to your church? Is telling others a part of your commitment when you accept Jesus as your Savior? Do you want to share Jesus with others? What are some ways that you can do this, either together as a group or as individuals? Are the baptismal vows important to you and do you want to do your best to honor them, God, and your church?

EXTRA GEM

Ellen White wrote about searching the Scriptures to find God's truth. Read what she wrote: "Do you ask, What shall I do to be saved? You must lay your preconceived opinions, your hereditary and cultivated ideas, at the door of investigation. If you search the Scriptures to vindicate your own opinions, you will never reach the truth. Search in order to learn what the Lord says. If conviction comes as you search, if you see that your cherished opinions are not in harmony with the truth, do not misinterpret the truth in order to suit your own belief, but accept the light given. Open mind and heart that you may behold wondrous things out of God's Word" (*Christ's Object Lessons,* p. 112).

Sharing Time

First Peter 3:15 isn't just a nice verse. It is a command. How can you prepare an answer to help you when others do ask about your faith? Write down some of the ways you can answer questions about your faith. What are some simple answers, and how would you answer more complicated questions? Don't be afraid if you don't know the answer, just say so and tell others you will look for the answer, and then do it. Knowing in your heart why you believe is important in making your faith your own.

Consider This

Review your baptismal vows this week. Or if you aren't yet baptized, look them over. Do you understand them? Are there some vows that you aren't quite sure about and need to review? Ask someone to help you so that you can understand them and make a renewed commitment to your church and to God.

My Uniqueness

loving me the way God made me

Youth are their own worst critics. The media today likes to present the message that they need to be perfect, but who decides what perfection is? God! He created each of you! Encourage your young people during this study to accept themselves as the wonderful people God made them to be. Compliments go a long way in the lives of youth!

Icebreaker

Ever hear the term *eagle-eyed?* It has become a catchphrase in many cultures and for good reasons. Most eagles have eyes that face forward. They have eyes so large that they cannot move them easily. So the eagle must turn its head to see to the side. That means eagles are forward-seeing. An eagle's eyesight is up to eight times better than that of humans. It can spot a rabbit or fish up to two miles away. Eagles also see in a great amount of detail. They can adjust the focus of their eyes at lightning speed. They keep a sharp focus as they swoop down from the sky and plunge in a fast dive toward their prize.

When eagles mate, they mate for life. They work together to build a nest that can reach up to nine feet in diameter and weigh up to two tons! The nesting pair will often return to this nest over and over, repairing and replacing it as needed. Since eagles can live up to 30 years in the wild, that's a lot of nesting seasons. Both parents guard the eggs in the nest. Their eggs are white and only slightly bigger than a chicken's egg. The eagle may start out small, but it becomes the king of birds.

The parents take turn bringing food to the young. The adults shelter the eaglets from bad weather and intense heat by covering them with their wings. As eaglets grow and take their first flight, the adult birds do not abandon their young. They often continue to bring them food and teach them hunting methods for up to one year.

Eagles do not usually eat carrion. What's that? you ask. It is otherwise known as road kill, or better yet, crow pizza. They hunt and fish for small game and fresh fish, preferring life-giving foods. But if an eagle does eat something that makes it sick, it does something interesting. It flies to the highest rock and goes spread eagle, letting the sun bake the poison out of it.

Dig In

We can learn some valuable lessons from the eagle. The Bible uses the strength and uniqueness of the eagle to teach us about our heavenly Father. And if we look closely, we can learn a valuable lesson about who we should be!

God made you as unique as He made the eagle. He created you with strengths, abilities, and choices. Like the eagle, we need to be forward-focused. We have to keep our eye on the goal before us and not let things around us distract us. That's not easy in this world of fast living. The only way to survive is to keep our eyes heaven-focused.

The eagle is thought to be "king of the birds." Do you know that God sees you in the same way? You are His crowning glory of creation. Yes, if you are like everyone else, you may not be perfect. But God wants to make up for that by infusing you with His character. Like the eagle's egg, you may start out small and plain, but God has a plan for you. A big plan—just like the eagle.

God stays close to us just like eagle parents. We are His children. He doesn't abandon us to the wolves. He teaches us and sets us free, but He is always close to watch and help and guide us until we learn we can't stand without Him.

Like the eagle, we often get desperate and do things that we know are not the right thing for us. What a lesson we can learn from the eagle. We need to go to the Rock, the highest Rock, and, like the majestic bird, spread eagle and let the Son bake the poison out of us.

Hot Potato

If you listen to the media you probably think that you are far from perfect. Unless you have a trim-and-fit figure or perfect nose, or wear the best of fashions, the media can easily convince you that you are not good enough. So you may constantly strive to make yourself better according to their standards. The problem is that you will never reach perfection according to the world. It's a constant chase, and if you ever did get to the end, you'd be pretty lonely there by yourself.

God created you just the way He wants you to be. He may have doused you with freckles, given you a silly laugh, or a bone structure that makes you not fit into a size small, but He is still the Master Designer. And He loves you without hesitation.

Hot Potato Questions

- Why is it so hard to look into the mirror and accept yourself the way God made you?
- Is everything about you a product of God's design, or are some things your choice?
- What ways do you wish you could be different? Can you do anything about these choices?
- Do you think it is OK for Christians to have surgery to change the way they look? (Things such as breast enhancement, altering features such as your nose or ears, face-lifts, etc.) Why yes or why not?

Bible Discovery

Psalm 139:13, 14. God knew you in the womb! Can you accept that God designed and planned for you before you were even born? How does a mother feel about the child in her womb? What things does she do to protect that child? Do you think that that is how God feels about you? If God thinks you are of value, shouldn't you feel that way, too?

Deuteronomy 32:10, 11. Have you ever felt that you were all alone in a desert land? Has the devil ever tempted you to look at yourself and think that you are not all you should be or reminded you of things that hurt you and make you think less of yourself? What does this verse say that God calls you? What does that phrase "the apple of his eye" mean to you? What do you need to do to see that you are the apple of God's eye? How can you help others to feel that way, too?

Deuteronomy 32:4, 31. Do you believe that God has a plan for your uniqueness in His world? Like the eagle, we have a Rock to turn to when we are in need. When you have listened to the poison that others may try to feed you about yourself, can you trust God to point you to His plan for you? Will God always be faithful when others fail you? Verse 31 essentially says, "My dad is better than your dad." Isn't it wonderful that you can boast this? God is not like any other father. He is faithful, and loving, and thinks you are the very best!

1 John 3:1. What word does this verse use to talk about God's love for us? "Lavish" (NIV)—what does that word mean to you? When you lavish, does it mean that you hold back something from what you are treating?

God doesn't hold back anything good from us. Do we ever hold anything good back from God? Do you think that accepting yourself is important to God? Could it make you different from the rest of the world? Would you be able to accept those differences and still be happy?

Isaiah 40:30, 31; Isaiah 40:28. How can you have the strength of an eagle? As a young person, why would you need this kind of strength while living in the world? The Bible says that your strength will be renewed if you hope in the Lord. Does the message of the world ever make you weary? Do you ever feel that you need God's message renewed in your life? Will God ever get tired of working for you? How do you know this? How can you listen more to God's message of acceptance—and soar like an eagle?

EXTRA GEM

Ellen White wrote about eagles, too. Read the following:

"In her endeavors to reach her home, the eagle is often beaten down by the tempest to the narrow defiles of the mountains. . . . At last she dashes upward into the blackness, and gives a shrill scream of triumph as she emerges, a moment later, in the calm sunshine above. The darkness and tempest are all below her, and the light of heaven is shining about her. She reaches her loved home in the lofty crag, and is satisfied. It was through darkness that she reached the light. It cost her an effort to do this, but she is rewarded in gaining the object which she sought. This is the only course we can pursue as followers of Christ. We must exercise that living faith, which will penetrate the clouds that, like a thick wall, separate us from heaven's light. We have heights of faith to reach, where all is peace and joy in the Holy Spirit" (*Messages to Young People*, pp. 102, 103).

Sharing Time

This week, find someone you know is searching for acceptance but is having a difficult time. Compliment them. Encourage them to see that they have worth in God's eyes. Look especially for someone that others might miss reaching out to. It may be hard to do this, but you will be blessing them and get a blessing in return.

Consider This

Take a good look in the mirror. Make a list of things that you wish you could change. Now, cross off of the list the things you can't do anything about. Copy on another page the things you can do something about. Make a plan to tackle them one at a time. Now, take the list of things that are crossed off and, in prayer, give them up to God. Yes, it may be difficult, but persist. Then, tear up the list and throw it away. You will have begun to accept the unique person God made you to be. And don't go digging around in the trash for those bits you have thrown away. Trust the God who created you perfectly!

New Ways of Evangelism
reaching the globe with technology

Young people are sometimes afraid to share their faith. Encourage them to look at new ways to do this. Remember that new technologies provide great opportunities to witness—but they also provide plenty of danger. Be wise and encourage them to work with their parents and other trusted adults when using the Internet and other technologies.

Icebreaker

Cash, cabbage, paper, dineros, dough, the list goes on. Whatever you call it—it still comes down to one thing: cold hard cash. We need it, we want it, and we use it. We keep it in our pockets, purses, wallets, banks, and sometimes under the mattress. It's hard to imagine a world without money, but as times get more difficult, we may have less of it. And that may drive more people to do something illegal—counterfeiting money!

In most countries, today's money is embedded and coded and produced in ways that make it quite difficult to imitate. Not so in earlier times. After the American Civil War, it has been estimated that between one third and one half of all U.S. currency in circulation was counterfeit! Some of the most famous bills sold in the North were of counterfeit Confederate dollars. These were clearly marked as copies and not legal tender, but since few could read, they passed for the real thing and almost collapsed the economy. In fact, in 1865, the United States Secret Service was started to deal with this problem.

Counterfeiting money is a felony in the United States. If convicted, you can receive a prison sentence of up to 15 years, along with enormous fines. And that doesn't apply just to paper money, either. Just try to make a coin worth more than five cents. You'll be subject to the same laws.

If you feel you must print funny money, make sure it's a different size than the real thing. Photocopying money is illegal unless it is larger or smaller than actual currency. It is also never intended to be "legal tender." With printers more and more sophisticated and people being people, this is the rule for those wanting to print something like a $1 million bill. And yes, it's been tried. Alice Pike tried to pay for her $1,671.55 charge at Walmart with one of three $1 million bills she possessed. A wise clerk called her boss, and Ms. Pike enjoyed the hospitality of the local Covington, Georgia, police headquarters. Then there was the guy in North Carolina who got away with passing a $200 bill and received $50 real cash in change. The bill—complete with George W. Bush's portrait—also contained text on the back such as "We like ice cream." He still hasn't been caught.

Dig In

You live in a world where everything has changed and is still changing because of new advances in technology. Unfortunately, the counterfeit of truth exists side by side with real truth. How do you know the difference, and what can you do to use technology to tell others about Jesus?

If you look, you'll find it. That seems simple, but it is true for almost anything you want to find these days. Want to learn something about your beliefs? You can find it and a thousand other pages on which people curse, belittle, and outright make fun of your convictions. The material is out there, so how do you sort the good from the bad? The best answer is to stay away from it. The devil is good at helping people take truth and turn it into error so subtle that you can get confused and afraid. Looking for this kind of material is looking for trouble. The best way to stay away is just that—stay away. Concentrate on telling the truth of the gospel. Opportunities abound for you to let others know that God is good and that they need a relationship with Him! (Leaders, make sure you also talk about the dangers of these technologies. Chatting with strangers can be a dangerous activity. Make sure you point this out even though they will tell you they know about it. Posting and chatting should be done only with the supervision of a parent and with their permission.)

The new mission field may very well be new advances in technology. You can fish the net faster than almost any other method of evangelism. You can reach people worldwide, and the good thing is that you don't have to be technically minded to do it! The Web has gone from just being computer screens to a place of relationships—just as the church isn't just buildings but people. The outreach of the Internet allows people to respond to each other, something we as humans need. And you can do it for other young people around the world right from your home computer!

All you need are people who will listen, and the Internet has plenty of them. Social networking sites have become extremely popular in the past few years. Blogs are often friendly and provide a sense of intimacy that young people crave. Blogs, videos, pictures, group discussions, are all ways that young people can share themselves with the world. So why not share the truth? Don't keep the beauty of what you have—share it with others.

Hot Potato

For some young people, sharing the gospel is hard. Why? Young people are often afraid of what others think of them, and it doesn't just mean on a personal level. Even with advances in technology—or perhaps more so because of it—sharing who you are and what you believe can be daunting.

But new technology provides a place where people can take what you have to say or leave it. It isn't the "in your face" kind of evangelism of the past. And it isn't a waste of time; it is an investment for God's kingdom. (Of course, you need your parents' permission before you post on any of the sites. Doing what they say is the right thing to do.) Everyone is sharing their opinion, so why not you?

Hot Potato Questions

- Have you used new technologies to share your faith? Why or why not?
- What methods have you used? Blogs, Web sites, social networking, texting? Do you feel that you have the knowledge to use the Internet to share the gospel? Why or why not?
- Have you checked into pages such as Yahoo Answers? Do you have a personal Web page on a site such as MySpace or Facebook? Is there anything on there about your faith?
- Are there things on your page that might make others question what you really believe?
- Why is it important to make sure your site reflects the true you and not a false sense of the world?
- How can you help others—your friends, your family, your church—develop sites or pages to share the good news? How do your parents feel about what sites you visit and what you post?

Bible Discovery

Mark 16:15. What commission did Jesus give His disciples? Is this commission still valid today for us? Why do you feel this way? Do you think that this verse applies only to missionaries in the field? Why or why not? Can new technologies reach most parts of the world? Can someone read something online that might peak their interest in wanting to know more about the gospel? Can sharing your faith in a simple, heartfelt way help others want to know Jesus more? (See Acts 1:8.)

1 Peter 3:15, 16. Why do we need to be prepared to share our "hope"? Have you ever had a chance to witness when you didn't think an opportunity would exist? If you post something online, will you get questions from others about what you have said about your faith? If you know what you believe and are grounded in your faith, will it help you to answer these questions better? Would others make malicious comments about what you post? How will you handle such comments? Will you strike back at them or do as this verse says? Can thinking about this now help you to handle the situation better if it arises?

Psalm 96:1-3. Does God like for us to praise Him? Why do you think this is? Can sharing our faith with others be a way to praise God? How can you best use the technology available to you to do this? What things has God done for you that you want to share with others?

1 Peter 2:9. Do you think that God has chosen you? Does that surprise you? Being royal means you are a child of the King. Isn't that amazing! Should you keep this news to yourself? Are there good and bad ways to share the gospel? Name some of the ways that might not always be appropriate to share with others. Name some of the ways that might be best.

Matthew 9:35-38. What do you think of Jesus' reaction to the crowds? He had compassion. Shouldn't we? What did He tell His disciples to do to help with the harvest of people? Should we also begin our evangelistic efforts with prayer?

EXTRA GEM

Ellen White knew that sometimes it is hard to share your faith. Read what she wrote to encourage us when we don't feel like sharing:

"Go to work, whether you feel like it or not. Engage in personal effort to bring souls to Jesus and the knowledge of the truth. In such labor you will find both a stimulus and a tonic; it will both arouse and strengthen. By exercise your spiritual powers will become more vigorous, so that you can with better success work out your own salvation. The stupor of death is upon many who profess Christ. Make every effort to arouse them. Warn, entreat, expostulate. Pray that the melting love of God may warm and soften their icebound natures. Though they may refuse to hear, your labor will not be lost. In the effort to bless others your own souls will be blessed" (*Testimonies for the Church,* vol. 5, p. 387).

Sharing Time

Think about what you have been sharing online on your personal space and with other technologies. In what ways can you change these to reflect God's glory? Think of something wonderful that God has done for you recently. Share it online with others in a way that would make them have positive feelings about God.

Consider This

This week, make a list of ways that you can share the gospel with others, whether in words or actions. Think of things that your youth group can do to witness to the community. Think of things your church can do. Leave tracts in odd places, such as the bank drive-through. Have a "parents night out" during which you babysit for a donation so that parents can have a few free hours together. Do a car wash just to witness and refuse donations. Give away cold bottled water at the beach with a "God Loves You" sticker attached. Start a CD ministry of Christian music and sermons.

Open your mind and you'll come up with dozens of ideas to get God's love out to the people who need it!

Peer Pressure
making ethical choices

Making ethical choices while experiencing peer pressure is hard for today's youth. Encourage them to feel free to discuss these issues while doing this Bible study. Provide a forum that is free from judgment.

Icebreaker

His name was Robert Wadlow. He was born in Alton, Illinois, in 1918. He was a good guy. He loved being a Boy Scout and didn't like attention. But in his short life, he got plenty of it!

By the time Robert was 10, he stood six feet six inches (198 centimeters) tall and weighed 220 pounds (100 kilograms). By the time he was 14, he had reached an astounding seven feet four inches tall. By age 18 he was more than eight feet tall. He wore size 37 shoes, too. In the mid-1930s they cost him an astounding $100. Doesn't sound like much in today's shoe market, but if converted to today's dollar, those same shoes would cost approximately $1,500. Robert wanted to study law and even enrolled in college. But to make ends meet, he signed a contract with the International Shoe Company in exchange for free shoes. He and his father embarked on a promotional tour. On July 4, 1940, they found themselves in Manistee, Michigan. The brace that Robert had to wear on his feet had caused a blister and then an infection. Doctors tried everything they could to save him, but he died 11 days later. At the time of his death Robert had reached the height of 8 feet 11.1 inches and weighed 439 pounds.

An overactive pituitary gland caused Robert's continual growth. No one knows how tall he would have been had he lived longer, but he still holds the record for being the tallest man that ever lived. (Of course, we know from the Bible that Adam was much taller, but the *Guinness World Records* people weren't around yet!) Robert truly lived above the crowd.

Not quite as tall as Robert? You can still rise above the crowd. Just buy a suite in Dubai's Burj Khalifa skyscraper completed in January 2010. It stands an amazing 2,723 feet (829 meters) above the exotic landscape of the United Arab Emirates and has 164 floors. Of course, the cost of buying might be prohibitive to most—the suites are selling for about $721 a square foot! Perhaps you will have to find another way to live above the crowd.

Dig In

The Bible talks about a young man who found a way to do just that. His name was Daniel. He and his friends were taken captive to a country very different from their own. Because of their superior intelligence and good looks, the king of that country thought it would be worth investing in their education. You remember the story. They were offered the best foods—or so the cook thought—from the king's table. But Daniel and his friends knew that the way they had been taught to eat was the best way for them. So they made a bargain and were allowed to follow their convictions. Daniel and his friends had to endure many challenges along the way. The pressure was enormous! If they didn't obey, they would face a fiery furnace and a night in a den of underfed lions. But armed with determination, faith, and the power of prayer, they met the challenges head-on. Though they were not spared the furnace, they were saved from its burning flames. And Daniel got to use a lion as his pillow for the night, because an angel kept the snarling beasts' mouths shut tight!

Hot Potato

Above the Crowd or Becoming a Chameleon?

Today young people face tremendous pressure to follow the crowd. Things that are habits for others might not seem right to you, but how do you fight against them? Technology makes this even more difficult than in times past. The instant broadcast of decisions through texting, the Internet, and cell phones takes gossip to a whole new level. Perhaps you find it easier to become like a chameleon by blending into your environment and adopting the things around you so you don't stand out in the crowd. But is that the wisest choice?

Most youth today would say that it is no big deal to cheat on a test, tell a white lie, or perhaps steal something from a local retailer. Everyone is doing it, right? No one gets hurt when you cheat on a test—or do they? Even in private schools, 64 percent of youth admit to cheating. Why? It may not be because of dishonesty or laziness. It may be because of pressure by friends to do so. Sound familiar?

Lying is another problem you probably see among your peers. It has become so commonplace that people accept it as normal and often don't even realize that a lie has been told. Have you ever told someone they look good, only to be thinking in the back of your mind that they are wearing the ugliest outfit you've ever seen? Have you ever exaggerated a story to make your peers think better of you, even when you know the details aren't what really happened? Lying grieves the heart of God because it is preventable. In His eyes, it is far from harmless.

Hot Potato Questions

- What is the issue you face the most peer pressure from in regard to ethical decisions?
- How do you stand against peer pressure when pushed to do things you know are wrong? Are you ever tempted to go against what you know is right just so you won't stand out in the crowd? Do you think there are things such as "white lies"?
- Why or why not? What can you do if you have made a mistake because of peer pressure? Can you make things right? Do you think God can forgive you?

Bible Discovery

James 4:7. What does the Bible tell us is the first step in combating peer pressure? How do you submit yourself to God? In what ways in your life do you see that you need to do this? Do you know that you can trust God for help in standing up against your peers?

Matthew 4:1-10; Matthew 16:1; Matthew 16:21-23. Jesus met pressure too, from the devil, the Jewish leaders, and His disciple Peter. How did He fight peer pressure? Besides Scripture, what other ways did Jesus use to help Him be strong against the things He was pressured with? What methods did Jesus use that you can apply to your life? How much time do you spend in prayer and Bible study? Do you think you could fit in more time for these important tools if you tried?

Matthew 26:41. What did Jesus tell His disciples to do to avoid temptation? Did they find this easy to do? What were the results of not doing as Jesus said? Did they later learn to do the things Jesus told them on that night? What were the results then? Can you learn from the mistakes the disciples made before Jesus' death and the triumphs they had afterward? How can you apply these lessons to your life, especially when it comes to the peer pressure you face?

2 Timothy 3:12. Is it reasonable to expect peer pressure in your life if you are trying to live right? Why or why not? What can happen as a result of being faithful to God when you are met with this pressure? Does growing ever not hurt? Is relying on God worth the cost of possibly losing friendships?

1 Corinthians 10:13. Do you believe this promise from Scripture? Why or why not? Has God proven Himself faithful to you when you are facing peer pressure? What ways can God provide for you to stand up against peer pressure? Are His ways limited or can He do things that we don't even think about? Is giving in to peer pressure ever right? Does it ever come without feeling guilty? What can we do if we make a mistake?

EXTRA GEM

Ellen White understood peer pressure. God showed her the challenge Daniel and his friends faced and their determination not to take a wrong step. Read what she wrote in *Prophets and Kings:*

"But Daniel did not hesitate. The approval of God was dearer to him than the favor of the most powerful earthly potentate—dearer than life itself. He determined to stand firm in his integrity, let the result be what it might. He 'purposed in his heart that he would not defile himself with the portion of the king's meat, nor with the wine which he drank.' And in this resolve he was supported by his three companions.

"In reaching this decision, the Hebrew youth did not act presumptuously but in firm reliance upon God. They did not choose to be singular, but they would be so rather than dishonor God. Should they compromise with wrong in this instance by yielding to the pressure of circumstances, their departure from principle would weaken their sense of right and their abhorrence of wrong. The first wrong step would lead to others, until, their connection with Heaven severed, they would be swept away by temptation" (p. 483).

Sharing Time

The hardest word in any language is no. Practice using it when faced with challenges by other youth to make unethical decisions. Look up

1 Peter 3:15 and memorize it. Remember to be ready with an answer for your faith, but do it in gentleness. You will then be able to help others make wise choices for good.

Consider This

Think about the past few months. Have you been pressured to make choices that don't fit into your ethics because of peer pressure? Write down the situations and how you responded. Now think of a response that fits into what God would have you do, and write that down next to your previous response. Keep the list handy so that when you face the temptations again, you will be ready with a response you can use to honor God and build up your faith!

Personal Devotion
quality time with Christ

Personal devotions is one of the most important steps a youth can take in developing their relationship with God. Encourage the young people to make worshipping God a habit, preferably in the morning. It takes discipline, but it is "food" that will make even the hardest days easier.

Icebreaker

Everyone loves a wedding with all its festivities and fun. Customs may be different in each country, but a wedding is a time to celebrate love. Of course, there are many things that lead up to that important day.

The engagement is often the first step toward a wedding. Of course, most girls will admit that they had been planning their wedding for years before Mr. Right came on the scene. But as soon as the asking is done, the planning begins in earnest. Did you know that almost 20 percent of engagements happen in December? Something about the holiday season, perhaps? The average engagement lasts 15 months. Perhaps that's because of all the planning involved! The busiest season for weddings in the United States is summer, followed by spring, and then fall. The least busy time for weddings is in the winter. Seems it's a great season to get engaged but not so for marrying. It may have something to do with the fact that the average American wedding costs an astounding $27,000! That would certainly eat up the "season of giving" budget.

Many traditional wedding customs date back centuries. For instance, the wedding cake has its origins in ancient Rome where guests would break a cake over the bride's head to symbolize fertility and abundance. In medieval times guests brought small cakes that they piled up on a table. The bride and groom would try to kiss over this pile. Someone finally got the idea of frosting them all together, and voilà—a new custom was born.

Of course, there are rules—written and unwritten—that must be followed as you proceed to holy matrimony. For instance, if you live in South Carolina, an old law on the books says that if a man proposes to a woman, he is legally obligated to follow through with that proposal. In Lebanon, Virginia, an old law states that it is illegal for a husband to kick his wife out of bed. It doesn't say that the opposite isn't allowed, so you have to wonder if they had an all-women city council.

After the wedding and the honeymoon—which in America costs an average of $4,500, and is most likely taken in the Caribbean, Hawaii, or Mexico—the real work of being married begins.

Dig In

Did you know that you have a special invitation to a wedding, too? At this wedding you are the guest of honor! And did you know that you are loved passionately? You are! Of course, the one who loves you so is your heavenly Father. He's crazy about you! He loves to lavish gifts on you, such as sending His Son for your salvation. He spends every day reaching out to you, hoping you'll reach right back. He wants to have a relationship with you that will be far more intimate than could ever be possible between two people. It's not just wishful thinking. It really can be that great. God's character is an open book. You can learn about it through His Word. Jesus came to show us who the Father is. What we see in the Son is also true for the Father.

So how can you develop this relationship with God? You've probably already started. You're at the right place—wanting to study His Word and apply it to all areas of your life. But like any relationship—without renewing and refreshing—love can grow stale. So what are some ideas to keep your love and relationship with God growing?

Don't forget to praise Him! Praise is the language of love between God and us. It honors God, and also is a strong weapon to help us during difficult times. Do it through prayer, music, and sharing what you are learning. Turn to His Word. Make it a definite part of every day. Did you know that if you read just three chapters from the Bible every day, you'll read through the whole Book in one year! Three chapters isn't much. But when you start, pray and ask for the guidance of the Holy Spirit. Then you'll have the opportunity to be open to what God wants you to learn. Find the best time for you. There's nothing better than starting the day with God. But if you aren't a morning person, don't let that keep you from God's Word. Anytime with God will be a great time! Don't forget to spend some of your time in prayer. Prayer means more than just talking; it also means listening. The more you grow in your relationship with your Father, the more you'll be able to hear His voice when He talks to you. That communication will become a delight in your life and will lead you even closer to Jesus.

Hot Potato

But what if you think you don't have time? Is it possible to be too busy to spend time with God? Of course! The devil's favorite tool is to keep us too busy to even think about our spiritual life. And it's not just extra things that take us away from spending time with God. There are plenty of ordinary daily things that interfere with our time.

Hot Potato Questions

- Do you already take time to have personal devotions? If not, what has stopped you from doing this in the past?
- Do you think it is important to spend some time with God every day? Why or why not?
- When is the busiest time in your day? When is the least busiest? When can you consistently carve out time to spend alone with God? Why would consistency matter in spending time with God?
- Do you think that God wants you to spend time with Him the way you do at work—punching in and out on the time card?
- Should devotion time be a choice rather than an obligation? Why or why not?

Bible Discovery

Psalm 119:9-16. Where does David say he hid God's Word? Was it easy for him to study Scripture? It's much easier today, isn't it? Can you hide God's Word in your heart if you don't read it for yourself? What other things did David do after he studied God's Word? (Leaders, he prayed and meditated on it.) What do you think David meant by meditating on God's Word? Is there a special place where you like to meditate on God's Word? Can you pray, praise, and meditate anywhere? Why or why not?

Psalm 5:3. When did David spend quality time with the Lord? Why do you think everyone emphasizes the morning as a great time to spend with God? Are you more relaxed in the morning or some other time? Why would that matter? When is the quietest time for you? That is a good time to have your devotions.

Colossians 2:6, 7. What does the Bible say you need to do after you have met and accepted Jesus into your life? How can you be "rooted" and "strengthened" (NIV) in your relationship with God? Can you rely on what someone else tells you that Scripture says or do you need to read it for yourself? Why? What does this verse say growing in that relationship will bring? Are you "overflowing with thankfulness" (NIV) for all that God is and does in your life? In what ways do you think you can be more thankful?

Ephesians 4:10-16. What will happen if you continue to learn more about God and His Son? Is maturity something to be desired in your faith? Why will maturing in your relationship help you love God more? What happens to others around you as you grow through personal devotional time with God? What do you think will eventually happen to you as a result of spending more time with God? Is that something to be desired? Why or why not?

EXTRA GEM

God showed Ellen White how important devotional time is to our lives. Read what she wrote: "Many seem to begrudge moments spent in meditation, and the searching of the Scriptures, and prayer, as though the time thus occupied was lost. I wish you could all view these things in the light God would have you; for you would then make the kingdom of heaven of the first importance. To keep your heart in heaven will give vigor to all your graces, and put life into all your duties. . . . As exercise increases the appetite, and gives strength and healthy vigor to the body, so will devotional exercises bring an increase of grace and spiritual vigor" (*God's Amazing Grace*, p. 295).

Sharing Time

One of the best ways to develop your time with God is to keep a devotional journal. Write down the verses that especially affect you and that you might want to share with others. Keep it with your Bible at all times along with something to write with. Whenever a thought strikes you, write it down. Someday you'll look back on these times and what you wrote and see how God has led you. It's also a perfect way to remember what you want to share with your friends and what questions you may want to ask your leader.

Consider This

Memorizing Scripture will help you feel more connected to God and His Word. Make it a habit this week to pick out at least one verse you would like to commit to memory. Write it in your journal and on an index card. Carry that card with you and work on memorizing this verse. You'll be surprised how easy it is after a while and how much it helps in your daily life.

Prayer
our 24-7 lifeline

Leaders, what a privilege you have to help your young people learn more about one of the greatest gifts they will ever receive, the gift of prayer. Lead them to this gift, and it will change their lives forever. Communication is the key to every great relationship, and it holds true with our heavenly Father. Prayer is a gift we have that will help us until the time we can speak with Him face-to-face.

Icebreaker

She can speak at an astounding 603 words per minute. That is 10 times faster than the average person. She's proven it twice for the *Guinness World Records* people. The last time was in 1990, when she spoke an astounding 603.32 words in 54.2 seconds! Fran Capo is known as the fastest-talking woman in the world. She also holds world records for the highest elevation book signing by an author (Mount Kilimanjaro) and the lowest elevation for a book signing (the wreckage site of the R.M.S. *Titanic* in a submersible). But it's the fast talking that she is most known for.

She discovered her unusual talent in the 1980s and has been at it ever since. The only problem with talking with her is that you can't get a word in edgewise!

Scientists have studied Fran and found that the Broca's area of her brain, the area associated with speech production, works extra efficiently. She uses a technique called "chunking," which means that instead of seeing individual words, she sees material in blocks. People that can do this are able to speak and memorize much easier. Linguists have also studied her speaking patterns and have learned that she speaks with certainty—using less tentative words such as "perhaps" or "maybe." She admits that coffee slows her down, and she says she can't function as well when she drinks it.

Dig In

Ms. Capo often uses the first two verses of Psalm 91 to demonstrate her remarkable talent. These beautiful verses read: "Whoever dwells in the shelter of the Most High will rest in the shadow of the Almighty. I will say of the Lord, 'He is my refuge and my fortress, my God, in whom I trust'"(NIV). These verses hold a promise for Fran Capo that she might not hear as fast as she says them. But you certainly can.

God wants to hear you speak too. But not like Ms. Capo does. He longs to talk with you in a gift that He has given us—the gift of prayer.

Prayer is a form of communication that we have with God. Just like in any relationship, communication is important. God chose prayer as a special link to Himself.

Scientists have actually studied prayer. They found that prayer helps in the healing process. Several studies have shown that even in blind prayer—where the subject does not know that they are being prayed for—unusual healing often takes place. As Christians, we already knew this. But is prayer more than just asking for healing and other things?

For Jesus, the answer was yes! One of the disciples came to Him and asked that He teach them how to pray. If Jesus' disciples needed to learn, maybe we do, too. He gave them an example that we can learn from. In Matthew 6:9-13 and in Luke 11:2-4 we are shown a special prayer that Jesus taught as a good pattern, something we call the Lord's Prayer. In it, we see that Jesus taught us to begin with praise. It is always good to praise our heavenly Father. Then, we are to ask that God's will be done in our lives. If we follow Jesus' example, we will ask for God's will before our own personal needs. Then we will talk to our Father about others, and how we can serve them and forgive. The part that many forget is to ask for protection and deliverance. The world is full of evil, and we need the protection and covering of prayer to overcome and remain faithful. Just as you wouldn't think about going into the battlefield without a weapon, you shouldn't consider trying to fight the war against evil without prayer. It is a proven and strong defense in this war. Then, we end as we began, bringing praise to our wonderful Father who loves us beyond our understanding.

Jesus let us know that there isn't just one way to pray. He spent hours of His earthly ministry in prayer. He prayed in quiet, peaceful places and in crowded synagogues. He prayed quick prayers. He prayed in agony on the cross and happily over the children gathered on His lap. He showed us that prayer is access to the Father—something every believer has the privilege of sharing.

But as in any good communication, prayer is not just about talking. It is also about listening. Communication must be a two-way street to be effective. Pausing in our prayers to listen for God's voice helps us to

grow closer to the Father and His will for our lives. The more you practice praying, the more your relationship with God will grow, and you will
come to hear His voice and know that it is your Father who is speaking.
Communication—to be good—must be practiced.

Hot Potato
All You Have to Do Is Ask!
Jesus said it right there in Matthew 7:7. Ask. Ask and it will be given to
you. So if Jesus said it, it must be true, right? Many people have taken Jesus'
words and done just that. Asked. Asked for things such as a million dollars,
or a new sports car, or the best gaming system out there. Why not? Jesus
said it. Others have asked for things such as the healing of a loved one, and
may have gotten the same answer as the prayer for a million dollars. Nada.
Nothing. Or so they thought.

Hot Potato Questions
- Does God answer these types of prayer? Is there a key to getting God
  to answer your requests no matter how outrageous or how heartfelt?
- What about the next verse (Matthew 7:8)? Does that help us better
  understand what Jesus meant?
- What are the things we should be seeking for in prayer? How do you
  know this?
- Does God want us to ask for His will for our lives? Is His will better than
  ours? Always? Does it sometimes not feel that way?
- Have you ever prayed and felt that God had not heard or answered your
  prayers? Did He do it later in His time?
- Do relationships matter with prayer? Will God answer prayer if you
  don't have a relationship with Him? Why do you think that way?

Bible Discovery
1 Peter 5:7. Do you have to carry your problems alone? No, God wants you
to come with all your problems and let Him take care of them for you. Do you
think you can trust God with everything that is on your heart? Why or why not?
Are there things you can tell your best friend, but not tell God? Why? He already
knows what is on your heart, so why can't you talk with Him about it?

Philippians 4:6, 7. How important do you think prayer is to God? Do you
think it is a vital part of a relationship with Him? Can someone that doesn't yet
know that they can trust God with anything still find comfort and strength in

prayer? According to these verses, how are we to come to God in prayer? What does thanksgiving mean to you? Does it mean that we are to believe that God will hear and answer our prayers in the best way for us, and we are to thank Him for it? Can we have peace in the middle of the hardest times in our lives? Can prayer help us do that? Does verse 7 give us that promise?

Psalm 62:8. How does David describe prayer in this verse? Why do you think he says that we should pour out our hearts to God? Have you ever cried and talked with a good friend when you were especially sad? Did you pour out your heart to your friend? Did they understand and try to help you? Do you think God wants to have that kind of relationship with you? David calls himself a tottering fence in verse 3. Have you ever seen a tottering fence or a leaning wall? Have you ever felt like David did? Do you think that God knows and understands and wants to give you the strength to stand upright again? Can coming to Him in prayer give you that strength? Why or why not?

James 5:17, 18. Can the prayers of just one person make a difference? It did in Elijah's time. Do you think it can still happen in our times? Why or why not? Elijah was a just man. Did he have a special relationship with God? Can we have that same relationship? If so, what are some of the ways we develop it? Is prayer on your list? Do you have to be at church to pray? Do you have to be on your knees? Do you have to pray out loud? Are there times that it is better to keep your prayers silent? (Leaders, sometimes we don't want to pray out loud because we want our conversation to be just with God and not let the devil hear what is on our hearts. Especially if we are praying for answers. This can be very important. Guide your youth in this discussion.)

Hebrews 4:14-16. How does God understand what we are up against in this world? Does Jesus understand temptation? When He was struggling on this earth, what did He do? Can we do the same? Will God give us strength, just as He did His Son? How does Paul tell us to approach God? What does that mean to you? Is the confidence that we should have the fact that God will hear and help? Do you have that confidence when you pray? Do you want to? How can you develop your relationship with your Father so that you can be confident when you pray?

EXTRA GEM

Ellen White knew that many people neglect the power of prayer. Read what she writes to encourage us: "The idea that prayer is not essential is one of Satan's most successful devices to ruin souls. Prayer is communion with God, the Fountain of wisdom, the Source of strength, and peace, and happiness" (*Child Guidance*, p. 518).

Here is another quote from Ellen White on prayer that should encourage you:

"It was in hours of solitary prayer that Jesus in His earth-life received wisdom and power. Let the youth follow His example in finding at dawn and twilight a quiet season for communion with their Father in heaven. And throughout the day let them lift up their hearts to God. At every step of our way He says, 'I the Lord thy God will hold thy right hand; . . . fear not; I will help thee.' Isaiah 41:13. Could our children learn these lessons in the morning of their years, what freshness and power, what joy and sweetness, would be brought into their lives!" (*ibid.*, p. 525).

Sharing Time

If you ask, people will respond to simple requests for prayer. With your youth group or with friends, go on a prayer walk. The only things you need are a small notebook and a pen to write requests. Pick a neighborhood that is safe, and go door-to-door and let people know who you are and that you are just out praying for the neighbors. Ask if they have anything they'd like you to pray about. You'll be surprised that very few people will refuse to pray with you or share a request. It is a wonderful thing to do on a Sabbath afternoon. Keep note of the requests. (You can return at a later date and check back to see how the requests were answered.)

Consider This

Start a prayer board. Use a corkboard, a small chalkboard, or just a notebook, but begin listing prayer requests that others share with you and those that are on your heart. Put a date by them as you begin to pray. Then leave room to write the date and answer to the prayer. Some will be answered faster than others, but all will be answered in God's time. It is a wonderful way to grow your faith by looking back and seeing how God has answered your prayers.

Premarital Sex
short thrill, long-term consequences

This is another hot topic study. Depending on the age and maturity of your group, you can adapt this study to their level. Cover this study with prayer. Do not be afraid to define the word "sex" within your group. Kids are having a hard time with this issue because they do not see some forms of sex as sex. Abstinence is talked about but not often defined, so youth may think that anything outside of penetration is acceptable. Do not be afraid to define God's plan for sexual relationship within the bounds of marriage—in all aspects.

Icebreaker

Everyone seems to love them—those who are willing to risk their lives for moments of thrill and entertainment. Whether it is jumping the Grand Canyon or free-falling from a great height, we are fascinated with watching people do things that resist the odds.

Jean François Gravelet-Blondin was one of those individuals. He was known as the Great Blondin. A French tightrope walker, he had a particular fascination with crossing the Niagara Falls gorge on a tightrope. And on June 30, 1859, he did just that—suspended 160 feet above the water. the rope was only three inches in diameter. In 20 minutes he walked from the United States to the Canadian side of the falls. Then he repeated that same act eight times over that same summer. He did it blindfolded, in a sack, trundling a wheelbarrow, on stilts, and carrying his manager on his back. He also walked the line and sat down midway, cooked an omelet, and ate it before continuing on his way. He returned again in 1860 and performed the stunt with hundreds of thousands looking on. Did he cheat death? He lived to the age of 73, which was impressive for his time (and profession).

In today's world there are still lots of tightrope walkers. Nikolas Wallenda is among the greatest. Working for several circuses, Wallenda continues a long family history of feats on the tightrope. In 1999 he proposed to his future wife, Erendira. But no ordinary proposal would do for this courageous man! In front of a crowd of onlookers, he walked out on a wire suspended 30 feet in the air, and got down on bended knee and asked his then girlfriend to marry him! He intends to walk across the Grand Canyon on a high wire to honor his great-grandfather, Karl, one of the original Wallenda performers.

Dig In

Today many youth are also tightrope walkers. They may not do 30-feet-up-in-the-air feats, but danger is still part of the walk. And it is encouraged everywhere they turn.

What is this rope that many are precariously walking? It is premarital sex.

Sex has many different definitions. The media certainly likes to make you think so. Everywhere you turn today, someone is trying to tell you that sex is OK outside of marriage. Postmodern thinking is that anything that feels right is right. It claims that there is no absolute moral truth. Television, the Internet, magazines, billboards, even other teens want you to buy into this thinking. Why? So they can sell you what they want to sell you, even if it cuts into your dreams and goals and provides only instant gratification. Don't sell yourself short! God's moral truth is still valid—especially for today's world.

Hot Potato

As young people, you are bombarded with lies about sex. Things such as "everyone is doing it." But are they? No. Not everyone. Studies show that only 25 percent of girls your age and less than 30 percent of boys are practicing any form of sex. While that number is way too high, if you are following God's plan for sexual relations (which means within marriage), then you are in the majority.

One of the lies you have to deal with is the new term *technical virginity*. That's someone's interpretation of the letter of the law. It's an excuse used by many teens for sexual activity. If you are "technically a virgin" (leaders, this means not having experienced penetration), then other sexual activity such as oral sex is acceptable. Many think that oral sex is safer. It doesn't lead to teen pregnancy, and you are less likely to get a sexually transmitted disease—at least that's what many think. But that thinking is flawed. HIV, human papillomavirus, herpes, gonorrhea, syphilis, chlamydia, and chancroid can all be contracted during oral sex.

Hot Potato Questions

- When President Clinton said that he had not had sex with Ms.

Lewinsky, he told the world that oral sex was not sex. If the president believes that, then why shouldn't you? What do you think? Is oral sex sex?

- How about other forms of sexual activity, such as masturbation or scarfing? Define sex.
- Many Christians feel that sex is defined by any genital contact, whether it is hand to genital, mouth to genital, or genital to genital. What do you think of that definition?

Bible Discovery

Genesis 2:24. What does it mean to become one flesh? Why do you think God created sexual union to bond two people? (Leaders, remind the youth that a bond means to unite, and the two become like blood relatives.) If sexual union bonds people, then wouldn't it make sense that it is to be saved for a marriage union, something you share with just one person? Notice the language used says a man and his wife. Is this God's plan for sex—in the beauty of marriage?

Song of Solomon 4:12. Song of Solomon is a beautiful description of love within a marriage. Some think it should come with a warning because it is so explicit, but do you think God wanted to share what His plan was for the beauty of a sexual relationship in a loving marriage? Why does this verse refer to the bride as being a sealed fountain or a locked garden? Are fountains and gardens good things? Are they best when they are meant to be shared? Do you ever fear that you will be alone? Does that ever tempt you to participate in things that should be saved for marriage? Do you think God understands this?

Matthew 5:28. What does Jesus tell us here about the letter of the law versus the spirit of the law? Define the word "lust." If lustful thoughts are sin, then why wouldn't lustful acts be sin? Can you perform any sexual act outside of marriage without lust being involved?

Romans 12:2. What does the media tell you about sexual behavior for teens? If you buy into this, are you conforming to the pattern of the world? How is God's pattern different? What do you think the renewing of your mind means? How can you make sure that you follow this? Have you found God's will to be good and pleasant? If not, what's holding you back from trying it?

2 Corinthians 5:17. Can sexual sin be forgiven? What assurance do you have of that? Many use the excuse that it is too late, so you might as well keep on doing what you are doing. But is it ever too late with Jesus? Does this verse give you hope if you have been caught in the trap of sexual sin? It should. God promises that you will be a new creation, the old is gone, which to Jesus means forgotten. God offers hope that is a sure promise, and He is always faithful! (See also James 1:17.)

EXTRA GEM

Ellen White understood about tightrope walking. Read what she wrote in a compilation called *Letters to Young Lovers:*

"Do not see how close you can walk upon the brink of a precipice, and be safe. Avoid the first approach to danger. The soul's interests cannot be trifled with. Your capital is your character. Cherish it as you would a golden treasure. Moral purity, self-respect, a strong power of resistance, must be firmly and constantly cherished" (p. 63).

Sharing Time

Many young people say that the reason they give in to sexual feelings is that they feel alone and hope that sex will help them feel less lonely. Do you know anyone like this? This week, think about your friends and seek out those who seem the loneliest. Build a friendship with them that will give them someone to talk with when they are troubled. Besides making a new friend, you may be giving them a chance to make a choice that will change their lives for the better. Be bold. Jesus will help you!

Consider This

This week, memorize the following verse and say it often. It will give you help if you fall into temptation. First Corinthians 6:18, 19 says, "Flee from sexual immorality. All other sins a person commits are outside the body, but whoever sins sexually, sins against their own body. Do you not know that your bodies are temples of the Holy Spirit, who is in you, whom you have received from God? You are not your own" (NIV).

Racism and Multiculturalism
our spiritual citizenship

Instead of getting better, racism is growing all over the world. People are growing apart in many ways. Help your young people see that God's way is to honor all people. They may have some strong feelings about this issue. Make sure you provide a safe environment for all to be heard.

Icebreaker
It started in the 1760s with John Spilsbury in England. Spilsbury was an engraver and cartographer. That simply means he made maps. Looking at a world map one day, he hit upon an idea. He quickly found a piece of hardwood the size of his map and then mounted the map to the hardwood. With a special saw used for making inlays, Spilsbury carefully cut out each individual country along its borders, and the puzzle was born. For more than 50 years the idea that had caught the public's attention remained for educational purposes only. It was a great tool for teaching geography.

By 1880, with the introduction of new types of saws, the jigsaw puzzle was born. Illustrations were glued or painted onto wood, and lines for cutting were penciled on the backs. Once cut, the puzzles could be put together not only to educate but entertain. In the late 1880s, another step in puzzle history began with the introduction of cardboard puzzles. And by the early 1900s special dyes were made to cut the puzzles with a press.

In the 1920s and 1930s the puzzle industry took off. The weekly puzzle was produced during the Depression era, and families gathered to spend time together and work at completing their puzzles. It was a cheap form of entertainment during hard times.

Today the puzzle industry is very much alive. And puzzles get harder and harder as the public demand for a challenge increases. No longer are puzzles only two-dimensional. High-tech puzzles have gone 3-D.

A man in Britain by the name of Ian Browncey spent more than 350 hours assembling one of the world's most difficult jigsaw puzzles. With 18,200 pieces, the puzzle is an astounding 6' x 10' picture of a jungle scene with more than 1,000 colors in it.

Dig In

You know the master puzzle maker. He has been at His craft for more than 6,000 years! Your heavenly Father has been designing intricate pieces that fit into His master puzzle, and He doesn't use a jigsaw. He creates wonderful people with individual personalities and gifts and tells us to work together to make the picture complete.

But there is one problem. We don't like to follow His direction.

Hot Potato

What's Wrong With This Picture?

We don't have the box to look at to see how the picture should come together, so sometimes putting the puzzle of our world together is difficult. But the problem doesn't lie only in not having the box; it is in our attitudes and dislikes. The problem has been around for thousands of years and instead of getting better, it is getting worse.

Racism. An ugly word that should be wiped from our vocabulary by now. But it hasn't been. Racism is growing throughout the world. And it isn't just a problem of different cultures or colors any longer. Whole nations have been attacked by divisions among national tribes. The Rwandan genocide of 1984 killed more than 800,000 people in just 100 days. The two warring tribes—the Hutu and the Tutsi—are part of the same country. They are in fact very similar—both speak the same language and follow the same traditions. Yet conflicts abound and racism almost caused the extinction of an entire tribe.

A new term has made its way into the mainstream society—*multiculturalism.* It encourages the keeping of one's heritage and culture. The proponents of multiculturalism don't support the melting-pot theory in which cultures blend together to make a new society, but they maintain that it is better for cultures and races to retain their roots and keep their individual culture and traditions alive. Some see multiculturalism as a way to end race conflicts, while others see it as a way to extend racism.

Hot Potato Questions

- Do you find racism and multiculturalism to be a problem in our ever-changing world? Why? Have you experienced the effects of either?

- Do you think it is important to understand and maintain one's own culture or do you think the melting-pot theory is better in the long run? Why do you feel this way?

- Do you think it is difficult to care about people different from you? Why do you feel this way? How do you think God wants us to feel and care about others who are different from us?

- What might be the danger in forming friendships with people of different cultures? (Leaders, God wanted the children of Israel to separate themselves mainly because of the different practices in religions and all that that entailed.)

- How can our young people guard against losing their own religious beliefs when forming friendships with others who have very different beliefs than their own?

- Should new immigrants in your country keep their own language and culture or be forced to adopt the culture of your country?

- Is there a difference between our physical citizenship and our spiritual citizenship? Could that help your thinking in this issue over racism and multiculturalism?

Bible Discovery

Genesis 1:27. Who is the Creator of all humanity? If all men and women came from Adam and Eve, aren't all people equal in the sight of God as offspring of Adam and Eve? Why do you feel this way? Do you think that God makes a distinction based on race or culture?

Genesis 11:1-9. Why do you think God chose to scatter people around the earth as a result of the building of the Tower of Babel? Why did confusing their languages make the people move to different parts of the earth? Do you think that God would give them the necessary changes to their bodies to adapt to the different areas they were living in? Would that include a gradual change in skin color? Should that have made a difference in how they began to treat each other? Why or why not? In our world today the barriers of language are bridged with technology. Do we let our lack of understanding another's language affect how we treat each other? Should we?

Romans 3:9, 10 and Romans 4:16, 17. Paul writes that all are sinners. What does he tell us in Romans 4:16, 17? Does he say that the promise of salvation is only for one group? If God promises that all people are given the free gift of salvation, why do we have such a hard time extending the same grace to others who are different from us? Is racism generational? Is it something groups pass down to their offspring? How do you think we can break the cycle of prejudice?

1 Corinthians 9:19-23. What do you think Paul means by saying "I have become all things to all people so that by all possible means I might save some" (NIV)? Should we sacrifice our own beliefs and customs to win someone to God? Do you think that is what he is saying? Did Paul mean that he studied people's customs and practices so that he would know best how to reach them with the gospel? Do missionaries use this method to reach the people that they are going to serve? The new approach to missions is to train "nationals"—people from their own country—to reach out where they live. Why do you think missions are starting to follow this line of approach? How can we accept others and their traditions and culture without giving up who we are? Can we become better people by learning about other cultures?

John 17:20-23. Whom was Jesus praying for in this part of His prayer? What does Jesus say that He wants us to experience? Can we do this if we have prejudice toward others? In verse 23 is Jesus saying that God loves us as much as He loves Jesus? Is that hard to believe? It is true. That is how much your heavenly Father loves you! As you come to grasp that, should it change how you look at others? Is it time to accept and love others the way God wants us to?

EXTRA GEM

Ellen White wrote the following on racism. See what she wrote:

"No distinction on account of nationality, race, or caste, is recognized by God. He is the Maker of all mankind. All men are of one family by creation, and all are one through redemption. Christ came to demolish every wall of partition, to throw open every compartment of the temple, that every soul may have free access to God" (*Christ's Object Lessons*, p. 386; *Ye Shall Receive Power*, p. 337).

Sharing Time

Sometimes the only way to stop something large is to take small steps. Each step counts. They may not all be the same, but it is the blending of them that makes for the beautiful patterns and that one odd piece that makes the whole thing work. This week, what can you do personally to help end a prejudice? If you want to make a difference in your generation, you'll have to contribute to the solution. Brainstorm some ideas that will show God's love for others, then make a positive step toward doing something to let others know their value to their heavenly Father!

Consider This

Look into your heart. Do you have personal issues with others because of their race or culture? Don't hide those in your heart. Pray about them and try to understand where they've come from. Make a list of your ideas, and with God's help see what you can do to accept others as He wants you to. Hiding a wound doesn't let it heal. God will help you if you ask.

Sabbath
a weekly gift

As a leader, you have no doubt come to realize our Creator's love for us in the creation of the Sabbath. Young people, with all their energy, may not yet see the Sabbath for the gift it is. Guiding them to learn more about the Sabbath will help them understand how to make good choices for making it the time of fellowship that God longs to spend with them.

Icebreaker

Imagine balloons, food, music, prizes, festive signs, maybe even fireworks. What comes to mind? Perhaps many things, but if we add in a big ribbon banner and a giant pair of scissors, does that help? Depending on where you are in the world, these are things usually accompanied by a grand-opening ceremony. Stores use this type of ceremony to announce to a community that they are opening their doors for service and they want to serve you! Other institutions often use this type of ceremony to show off their new facility—a school, a hospital, maybe even a new factory. Everyone is in a celebratory mood with high hopes for the future of their endeavors.

Perhaps the most famous of grand openings are the Olympic ceremonies: the world literally celebrates with festivities viewed by millions. These ceremonies have become a tradition of extravagance.

The Olympic opening ceremony held for the 2008 Beijing Summer Games was watched by almost 100,000 in attendance at the "Bird's Nest" stadium, and by millions more around the world via television. The four-hour ceremony was one of the most elaborate and most expensive of all the opening-ceremony shows. It is estimated that the show cost more than $300 million to produce, with more than 15,000 performers. In attendance, along with leaders of several countries, 11,000 athletes represented 204 countries around the world.

One of the most spectacular moments came when the fireworks lit the night sky. Twenty-nine giant footprints filled the air. Most watching live and on television were thrilled at the sight as the footprints led from Tiananmen Square to the stadium. Only later was it revealed that the only footprint firework that was real was the one just outside the stadium. It was a clever work of computer graphics inserted into the live coverage at the correct moment.

Dig In

Did you know that the Bible talks about a grand opening day, too? It's right there in Genesis. God created the Garden of Eden, then man and woman, and put them in that wonderful place. For the ribbon ceremony, God created a river that wound through the garden and watered it. Birds of all colors filled the sky more beautifully than any balloons or fireworks ever could. It was a festive, wonderful day—humanity's first full day on the new earth—and Adam and Eve spent it with their Father. What was this marvelous day? The Sabbath!

We can only imagine what that day was like. Humanity walking face to face with God. Perfect creation everywhere. Imagine the angels looking on at the celebration—oh, there certainly had to be music in the air! What a day that first Sabbath had to have been. The best grand opening ever!

Hot Potato

The Lord's Day or the Law's Day?

Then sin entered the world. And here's where the story turned ugly. Adam and Eve had to leave their garden home. No longer could they walk and talk with their Father face to face. Imagine their broken hearts!

But God allowed them to take the Sabbath with them when they left their garden paradise. A souvenir to keep from that spectacular grand opening. We still have that jewel still left from our Eden beginnings: the Sabbath.

We don't know exactly what God did with Adam and Eve on that first Sabbath, but we do know it was meant as a celebration of His creation. It was a festive day. Perhaps they walked through the garden marveling at each part of its incredible beauty. They talked and they feasted. It was a time of joy. There weren't rules yet on how to keep the Sabbath, and they weren't needed, because the Creator of the day walked with them.

It didn't take humankind long to change all that. Soon the Sabbath went from being a blessing to being a burden. The devil likes to make things happen that way—to take the gifts of God and turn them into something He never intended. And we are good at following right down his trail!

Hot Potato Questions

- When you look at that first Sabbath in Eden, how far do you think we have come from what God intended the day to be?
- Give specific examples. (Leaders, be ready with some suggestions to help get the discussion started.)
- Do all of humanity's rules for the Sabbath ever make you feel it is more of a burden than you want to be a part of? Why or why not?

Bible Discovery

Genesis 2:1-3. What two things do these verses mention God did on the seventh day? Do you think God "rested' because He was tired? In Hebrew, this term means that He ceased (creating). Does that change anything for you? When you make something beautiful, what do you do when you finish? Do you take time to look at it and celebrate your creation? Do you think that was what God was doing? What things do you think God shared with Adam and Eve on this first full day of their lives? How can you apply that to your worship on the Sabbath?

Isaiah 58:13, 14. What did God Himself call the Sabbath? God used the word "delight." Many people don't feel that the Sabbath is any kind of a delight because of what humanity's has done to it. "Holy" means set aside for God, not set aside for rules. In what ways do you find the Sabbath a delight? In what ways is the Sabbath not a delight for you? Is there anything you can do about that?

Mark 2:23-28. What did Jesus call Himself in these verses? Why were the Pharisees complaining about the disciples? Did Jesus have a problem with His disciples picking the grain and eating it on the Sabbath? What does that tell us about how we can honor God on His day? Do you think that meeting our needs is important to God? Can we help others with their needs on the Sabbath? What things can you do to honor God and help others with on the Sabbath? (Leaders, youth may be afraid to speak out for fear of being wrong. Encourage them to share their thoughts and make a list of them on a chalkboard or poster.)

Luke 14:1-6; Luke 4:16; John 5:1-14. What things do these verses tell us that Jesus did on the Sabbath? It mentions that He was dining, going to a feast, fellowshipping, healing, and worshipping! What can we learn from

Jesus' example that God intended for us to do on His day? Make a list of things that you think are appropriate for the Sabbath and compare them to Jesus' example. How do you think they fit in with God's plan? What things would you definitely not do on the Sabbath because you think they would not be in keeping with the day? Why? Do you ever get caught up in honoring the day and forget to honor your Maker?

Exodus 16:23. What were the Israelites told to do to prepare for the Sabbath? The promise of manna was tied to their choice of celebrating the Sabbath, if they believed there would be ample food for their needs. Notice the word "keep." What does that word mean to you? Don't you keep the things that are a treasure to you? Do you think God feels that same way about you? Do you think that might be why He wants us to spend the day in celebration, worship, and fellowship with Him and other believers?

EXTRA GEM

Ellen White writes the following about the beauty of the Sabbath: "God is merciful. His requirements are reasonable, in accordance with the goodness and benevolence of His character. The object of the Sabbath was that all mankind might be benefited. Man was not made to fit the Sabbath; for the Sabbath was made after the creation of man, to meet his necessities. After God had made the world in six days, He rested and sanctified and blessed the day upon which He rested from all His work which He had created and made. He set apart that special day for man to rest from his labor, that, as he should look upon the earth beneath and the heavens above, he might reflect that God made all these in six days and rested upon the seventh; and that, as he should behold the tangible proofs of God's infinite wisdom, his heart might be filled with love and reverence for his Maker" (*Testimonies for the Church*, vol. 2, p. 582).

Sharing Time

Define the things you think are appropriate for a day of celebration, worship, and fellowship with God. Do you think these fit in with humanity's ideas? The Jews had a rule that they couldn't carry their handkerchief on the Sabbath unless it was pinned to their robe on Friday before sunset. Many people think that Seventh-day Adventists keep the Sabbath in these same ways. Think of someone you can share with who needs to learn the beauty of the Sabbath and share with them some of the things you do to "keep" this treasure of a day.

Consider This

After studying about the Sabbath, do you have new ideas about what God intended the day to be? Write a letter to God about what the Sabbath means to you, expressing how you want to find the delight that God intended the day to be. Pray as you are writing and listen for the voice of your Creator as He shares in your delight over this marvelous gift.

Sanctuary
then and now

Leaders, this study on the sanctuary is meant to show the young people that they can understand things that seem very hard. It is also a message about salvation. Pray for your young people!

Icebreaker

As he picked up his ax from the tent floor, he again had to ask himself if he was crazy. Crazy? But he had spent enough time talking with God and walking with Him to know His voice. They were close. Their relationship was not one-sided. He knew that. But still, this? This?

He walked to where the wood waited. Raising his ax, he split the wood in two, making perfect pieces for the fire. Was he crazy? No. God asked. He knew enough to trust Him. He stacked the wood in bundles and tied them onto the donkeys. He was 120 years old. Yet he wouldn't let anyone else do this most menial of tasks for this sacrifice.

He knew about sacrifice. He knew that it pointed forward, a foreshadowing of things to come. Mighty things. Wonderful things. Unspeakable things. He knew that it had been committed to Father Adam, the knowledge of God's law and His government. He knew about the sacrifice to come. And He held on to that promise even as he picked up the gleaming knife and tucked it into his belt. But how did this sacrifice fit in with the one to come? How?

They walked. The silence was broken only by the sounds of nature around them. His heart was too heavy for the words he longed to speak. At night, they looked to the sky, and he was reminded that more than 50 years ago the promise of this heir that now sat beside him was given. And God always kept His promises. Always. So was he crazy now? No. He wouldn't listen to the voice that told him so. He knew God's voice, and this whisper in his ear was not God's voice.

Three days. Little sleep had worn him down, but the sight of Mount Moriah and the cloud of God's glory hovering over it gave him new strength to trust that the heavenly messenger had been correct. He clung tightly to the promise that this son, this miracle, would be the father of nations. The promise had come from God. Surely

God could raise his son from the sleep of death. He wasn't crazy. He believed.

They went up the mount alone. No, not alone. God was with them. At the top his son paused, asking the question "Look, the fire and the wood, but where is the lamb for a burnt offering?" Then he replied with the promise of God, "My son, God will provide for Himself the lamb."

Dig In

Fast-forward about 250 years. The promise of God to Abraham hasn't yet been fulfilled. God's lamb was provided that day on the mountain, and by faith he had believed that all God's promises would come true. In God's time. But now, the children that God had called to be His people were wandering in the desert. Years of slavery had forced them to forget about God's sacrifices. The superstitions about animals held by the Egyptians they served didn't allow for them to make the sacrifices God required. Without this foreshadowing, God's children had forgotten too much. So God gave Moses a perfect pattern, a miniature of the heavenly sanctuary, to remind them about God's plan of salvation that was to come. God wanted to come and dwell with His children, so He wanted them to have a place here on the earth that would remind them of heaven, and what it would cost Him to have His family home with Him: the death of His only Son. Something Abraham had understood on several levels.

Hot Potato

Type Versus Antitype

Type, antitype. You've heard those words many times, but have you ever figured out what they mean? It's really quite simple, at least on the surface. It means symbol meets reality. The symbol of the sacrifice in the sanctuary pointed forward, foreshadowing—another big word that's used a lot—to Christ's ultimate sacrifice on Calvary. With that in mind, the sanctuary and its symbols become much easier to understand. Also, the beauty of the whole system becomes clearer. What an awesome God we serve!

Understanding and applying the sanctuary service in our lives is what makes us uniquely Adventist. Many think it is the Sabbath, but several other denominations also know the truth about honoring God's holy day.

Adventist Christians are the only ones that apply the sanctuary's meaning to God's salvation. Shouldn't we take the time to study it more and discover the meaning and beauty of God's perfect plan?

Hot Potato Questions

- Have you spent much time studying the sanctuary message? Why or why not?
- Have you stayed away from learning about it because you were afraid it would be too hard to understand?
- Do you see how the sanctuary here on the earth is a miniature of the heavenly one?
- Does that make you excited to know more about its structure and mission?
- Can you see how the sacrificial system pointed forward to Christ's sacrifice?
- Why do you think it is important to know that Jesus is ministering now in the sanctuary for us?

Bible Discovery

Exodus 25:8, 9; Hebrews 9:1. Why do you think God was so exact in His details to Moses for building the first earthly sanctuary? Does it tell us anything about His character and His love for us? What do you think it must have felt like knowing that God's glory was going to be there in the tabernacle? Does it make you think about heaven and what it will be like to worship God face to face? How did the rituals of the sanctuary service fit into the first covenant? We often look at rituals as being lifeless and old. Do you think what God asked the priests and the people to do in the sanctuary became archaic and old to them? Do you think they forgot about what the service pointed toward? Do we sometimes forget what Jesus has done and is doing for us?

Hebrews 8:7-13; Jeremiah 31:34; Hebrews 8:1, 2. Why did God make a new covenant? What had humanity done to annul the first covenant? Did they find it hard to worship God only? Why do you think it was so hard for mankind to keep God's covenant? How would sending Jesus assure that the new covenant would not be broken? Does the new covenant include a sanctuary?

Revelation 15:5; Hebrews 8:1, 2; 1 Timothy 2:5. What did John see in his vision? Does the heavenly sanctuary include a priest? How did the priests in the sanctuary mediate the sins of the people? Does the priest's role as mediator show the seriousness of sin? Did placing their hands on the head of the animal before sacrifice transfer their sins to the animal symbolically? Did the true Lamb on the cross transfer our sins to Himself?

John 1:29. Who did John say Jesus was? Do you think he understood what Jesus had come to do? Do you think that the people of John's time were still looking forward to a Savior, or had the sacrifices again become routine? Did the Lamb of God end sacrifices with His death on Calvary? Did the people understand that Jesus was the foreshadowed lamb? Do you think it is easier today to understand, having the complete Bible for our study? Do you think you should spend more time in God's Word learning about the sanctuary?

Hebrews 4:14-16. How do you think Jesus is ministering for us today in the sanctuary? What is He trying to achieve for us? Another of the big words we often toss about is "atonement." If you break it down you can see its meaning, "at one ment." Its simple meaning is reconciliation. God wants to be at one with us, and He can do this through the work of Jesus. The sanctuary is Jesus' command center, to put it in easier terms. It is from here that He is working for us. Does Jesus understand how hard things are for us? Do we have the promise that He sympathizes with our weaknesses? Is it hard to love God, knowing what He sacrificed for us and what He even now is doing to make heaven possible?

Hebrews 9:28; Ephesians 1:4-10. What will happen at the end of Christ's ministry in the sanctuary? When He comes again, will we be the reward for His sacrifice? Does that humble you to know that that is how God feels about you? In the earthy sanctuary, what do you think is meant by the symbolism of the scapegoat? Whom does it represent? What will be the final end of the scapegoat? Will sin finally be banished forever? Then and only then can all things be brought together in Christ. Wow. What a hope we have. Does that make you want to know more?

EXTRA GEM

Ellen White encourages us to study about the sanctuary. Read what she wrote: "We should be earnest students of prophecy; we should not rest until we become intelligent in regard to the subject of the sanctuary, which is brought out in the visions of Daniel and John. This subject sheds great light on our present position and work, and gives us unmistakable proof that God has led us in our past experience. It explains our disappointment in 1844, showing us that the sanctuary to be cleansed was not the earth, as we had supposed, but that Christ then entered into the most holy apartment of the heavenly sanctuary, and is there performing the closing work of His priestly office, in fulfillment of the words of the angel to the prophet Daniel" (*Maranatha*, p. 247).

Sharing Time

Sometimes we put off studying things we think are difficult. Since the sanctuary study makes us unique in the Christian world, shouldn't we be prepared to share its beautiful message with others? Write out a short and simple message that sums up the sanctuary so that you will be prepared to share it with others. Work together, but keep it simple. The message and symbolism can be very deep, but it can also be explained simply. Working on this before you have to present it will help you be ready when the opportunity comes to share.

Consider This

Do you understand the sanctuary message to be one of salvation? Have you asked for and received God's promise into your life? Take time to ask for God to become the Lord of your life. From the beginning, He has planned for you to be a part of His kingdom. If you haven't asked Him to do that, what's stopping you? If you have, then recommit your life to Jesus and share the message with others. God wants us to share this good news with everyone in the world!

Second Coming
a day of glory and hope

Fear. It's the reaction most young people have when they think about the Lord's return. Studying about it will help them understand that God will help them through the hard times. They also need to understand the culture around them and why most people want to believe in the secret rapture. Then they can share what they believe to help others understand.

Icebreaker
Fire Flowers

Whether it is the Dahlia, the Willow, the Chrysanthemum, the Ring, or the Spider, people around the world can't get enough of them. What are we talking about? Fireworks, of course.

China is recognized as the birthplace of fireworks. About 2,000 years ago the Chinese invented Chinese crackers, a mix of gunpowder that provided a loud bang. These firecrackers were used to celebrate weddings and births, and were thought to scare away evil with their noise. It wasn't long before other nations developed their own version of these exploding beauties. India and Thailand used them for centuries to celebrate their ceremonies. They attached rockets to bamboo sticks, some as long as 40 feet, and lit them off to celebrate.

At the 1486 wedding of Henry VII, the sky was alight with the exploding orbs. Queen Elizabeth I even created a position in her court—fireworks master—so that there would be a person in charge of organizing displays for important occasions. One such master was even knighted for his amazing display for the coronation of James II.

The first fireworks recorded on American soil were set off by Captain John Smith. And that tradition continued with the inauguration of George Washington. Today millions of dollars of the glowing beauties are used to celebrate American Independence Day on July 4.

The first fireworks were all about the bang until the Italians began experimenting with chemical compounds and trace amounts of metal. Finding that these additives created amazing bursts of light changed the industry. In the early 1800s the science of modern fireworks with all the bang and colors began.

Whatever the celebration, people around the world look forward to watching the exploding lights. Wherever your seat, you can't miss them illuminating the night sky.

Dig In

We love to watch these exploding beauties, but is there a cost for these momentary pleasures? Unfortunately, yes. Thousands around the world are injured each year by them. And more than half the injuries occur to children age 14 or younger. Sixty-three percent of the injuries sustained are from burns—mostly to the hands, eyes, and faces of those looking for a little excitement. What seems like the most harmless of these powerful explosives is actually the one that causes the most damage: sparklers.

Hot Potato

Can't Hide It Under a Bushel

Wherever their light is twinkling, fireworks can be seen for miles around. Once lit, there is no denying their power and beauty. For miles around, every eye can enjoy the sight of their magnificent light and sound.

Just as fireworks are for every eye, Jesus promises to return in an unmistakable way. His first coming to the earth was without the fanfare of His final triumphant return. The prophecies had been there for hundreds of years, but only a few shepherds, a handful of faithful-hearted people, and some night-sky watchers who traveled at great length to see the baby king were witness to His first coming. A choir of angels was the only noise that accompanied His birth. It won't be the same for His second coming.

So why do some believe that His coming will be quiet and seen only by a few? A popular series of books has been written on the subject to entertain and draw young people to this belief in a secret rapture. But what does the Bible say about it? The answer is nothing. There is no verse at all that speaks of Jesus' second coming as something that will be secret.

The verses that some like to use are found in Luke 17:30-36. If you read the entire section starting with verse 20, the answers are quite clear. Jesus explains it Himself. He talks about how it was in Noah's day first. The people were warned by an old man building a boat, and they laughed and partied right up until the first raindrops fell. God didn't leave them without warning. They didn't have the faith to believe. Noah's sons and their wives did, however, and they entered the ark and were saved. The rest pounded on the door of the ark as the water rose and were drowned. Then Jesus mentions the days of Lot. The people were warned, but again, they continued their lifestyle until the first hailstones fell. Lot and his daughters left the city and were saved. The rest of the inhabitants died in the ensuing destruction.

It will be that same way when Jesus comes again. The Bible is clear on that. There is no secret rapture—just two groups of people. Those who listen to the warnings and are prepared for Jesus' imminent return, and the other group—those who will not be ready and will continue their ways until they see that tiny cloud in the sky become brighter and brighter as Jesus speeds to the earth to take His loved ones home. They will die by the brightness of His face and the glory of His presence.

Hot Potato Questions

- Why do you think people are so mixed up about Jesus' return? Do they want to believe what others tell them, instead of studying God's Word for themselves? Do you think they want to believe it will be this way to avoid the hard times that will happen on the earth just prior to His coming?
- How will anyone be able to live during the last plagues? Will God's people have special protection? Why do you believe this way?
- Does Satan love to offer a counterfeit to get people mixed up about the truth? Is he good at this?
- What can we do as God's children to prepare for Christ's second return? Should we focus on how hard the times will be or spend our energy in telling others about the good news of salvation? Why do you feel this way?

Bible Discovery

Acts 1:1-11. The Bible is clear that Jesus spent 40 days with His disciples after the Resurrection. They watched as He was physically taken away from them. What did they do then? Why do you think God sent two angels to deliver a message to them? What did the angels promise? Did they say that the Jesus they knew—the flesh-and-blood Jesus—would indeed return to them at His second coming? Is this a promise that we all can take to heart? (See also Luke 24:36-43. Jesus is a personal God, not just a spirit.)

Revelation 1:7; Matthew 24:30. John was shown the second coming of Jesus. Who did He say would see Him at His return? If every eye is to see

Him, then how could the saints already be raptured? Jesus' return will be very visible to all. Jesus Himself tells us that all will see Him and will hear the angel's trumpet blast. His coming will be visible. Can you take comfort in the words that Jesus said Himself?

1 Thessalonians 4:16. Does the Bible tell us that Jesus' return will be quiet? How does this verse describe what will happen when Jesus returns? Why do you think Jesus will come with a loud shout? How do you feel when you see someone you love after a long absence? Do you give out a shout when you see them coming toward you? Do you think that is how Jesus feels about us? (See also Matthew 24:31.)

Luke 21:8, 9; 1 John 4:2, 3; 2 John 7. In these verses the Bible warns us about what? Have there been people in recent years who have claimed to be a savior? How does the Bible say that we can know whether someone is from God? Why would false prophets deny that Jesus had come in the flesh? Would they then have to claim that He also will come again in the flesh? What do you think are the best ways to stay strong against the crazy things that will go on around us during the days just prior to Christ's second coming?

Matthew 24:32-35; 2 Peter 3:8-10. What lesson can we learn from the fig tree? In spring, when you see fruit trees blossom, do you know that the fruit is coming? Can you look around you at the things happening in this world and know that Jesus' return has to be soon? Is God's timing different from ours? What do we have to do to make sure we don't get discouraged as we wait for the Lord to return? Do you think it will be worth the wait?

EXTRA GEM

Ellen White wrote words of encouragement and warning for us about Christ's return. Read these two passages from an article first published in the *Review and Herald:* "Now is the time to prepare for the coming of our Lord. Readiness to meet Him cannot be attained in a moment's time. Preparatory to that solemn scene there must be vigilant waiting and watching, combined with earnest work. So God's children glorify Him. Amid the busy scenes of life their voices will be heard speaking words of encouragement, faith, and hope. All they have and are is consecrated to the Master's service" (Nov. 13, 1913).

" 'So shall also the coming of the Son of man be.' The people will be eating and drinking, planting and building, marrying and giving in marriage, until the wrath of God shall be poured out without mixture of mercy. Men have been taught by their ministers to believe that the coming of Christ is to be spiritual, or is to take place in the distant future, and the message of His soon return has been denounced as fanaticism or heresy. Skepticism and 'science falsely so called' have undermined faith in the Bible. The multitudes are striving to forget God, and they eagerly accept fables, that they may pursue the path of self-indulgence undisturbed. The people are hurrying to and fro, the lovers of pleasure intent upon amusement, the money-makers seeking wealth; and all are saying, Where is the promise of His coming?" (*ibid.*).

Sharing Time

Many young people have been caught up in the popular book series describing the second coming as a secret rapture, because they want to avoid thinking about how hard things will be during those days. Now that you have studied the truth about Jesus' return, what promises from Scripture can you share with your friends to help them know that God will not leave them during those difficult times? Make a list of verses to share with others, and do so this week.

Consider This

Are you discouraged about the things going on around you? Are you afraid that things will get worse? The Bible tells us that the times around Jesus' return will not be easy. But it also gives us promises that we are not to fear. Memorize Scripture texts this week that bring you hope when you are afraid. Write out at least two verses on index cards and commit them to memory. Then you will have ready strength to draw on when you need it most. (Luke 21:28 is a good place to start.)

Sexuality

protecting God's temple

This is a sensitive subject that may make some of the youth uncomfortable in a group setting. Be aware of the needs of your youth when presenting this topic. They probably know more than they will let on. Make sure you know all the terms used in this study. You as the leader should know the maturity of your youth. You can take this study deeper if it is appropriate, or leave it at surface level.

Icebreaker

Got to Love 'Em!

Everybody loves good old home-style cooking. Whatever the culture you come from, or whatever your favorite foods are, a big, satisfying meal is a comfort to almost everyone.

Americans celebrate Thanksgiving in late November. It is a holiday steeped in tradition and, unfortunately, indulgence. Most cooks spend hours preparing food that couldn't possibly be devoured in one meal even if they invited the whole neighborhood to their table! In fact, the average Thanksgiving meal contains about 3,000 calories and 229 grams of fat! No kidding. That's about three times the recommended fat-gram allowance for someone your age in a single day. You'd have to walk 30 miles to burn up those calories!

Another occasion to feast occurs at the buffet line. The modern buffet started in France in the eighteenth century. Sweden offered their version with the smorgasbord, which literally means "table of sandwiches." No matter where you are in the world, you can enjoy wonderful dishes you can choose from—again and again. Buffet restaurants seem to be springing up everywhere these days. Around the world, people can't seem to get enough of these places where they can pay one price and eat all of the food they can manage. And boy, do they! The average person eats up to 4,000 calories at one of these places. And that figure seems to be on the low end of the scale. It is not unheard-of to consume up to 10,000 calories at the buffet line. Some figures suggest hearty eaters chow down to the tune of 13,000 calories in one guilty pleasure. Scary, huh?

Dig In

Buffets are popular because of the variety of foods offered and how there seems to be something for everyone. Most people take stock of the offerings, then plan how to fill their plates.

Can you eat healthfully at a buffet? The answer is yes. There are lots of good choices. Most buffets include a salad bar and lots of fresh veggies and fruits. But most people don't make good choices.

Today's youth have a different buffet set before them. Enticing, inviting, indulgent choices that seem hard to walk away from. The variety may astound you, actually. You are probably aware of most of the items at this buffet. To start, there's "sexting." Then there is cutting and masturbation. Pornography and fingertip porn are as easy as logging on to the computer. More items can be added, such as scarfing, but by now you probably get the point. Today's teens have a buffet line of sexual temptation that is confusing, daring, and frightening.

Just as you choose what you eat at a buffet, you control what happens at the sexual smorgasbord set before you. The choice is yours. You control your habits and thoughts. You can make wise choices that will affect your life for years to come, or not. But help is available in making those choices. God has provided a lot of wisdom in His Word. You just need to choose it.

Hot Potato

One of the problems youth face is their failure to choose wisely. Giving in to gratification is easier than fighting against the hormones raging in your bodies. The confusing messages sent by the media don't help either. Seeking personal pleasure as your God-given right is a message constantly thrown at you. Everyone is doing it, after all. You want to fit in, so what's wrong with seeking something you feel is missing in your life? And the media (and maybe your friends) are quite good at telling you that pleasure is the thing you are missing and sex is just the ticket.

Hot Potato Questions

- Do you know which group accesses the Internet for pornography the most? Studies show that it is conservative Christians.
- And the age group that uses the computer for porn the most? Those 12 to 17 years old. Does this surprise you?
- Is it a double standard? Viewing sexual material and participating in things such as masturbation isn't like having sex, right?

• Are you still a virgin after doing these things?

Bible Discovery

1 Corinthians 6:19, 20. Is your body really your own? What was the price paid for your body? Does that price make a difference in how you treat it? Why or why not? As a Christian, do you think that this verse refers to what you eat and drink only, or does it include things such as sex, what you watch on TV, or things you read in magazines? How could these other things affect your body?

1 Corinthians 6:12. What do you think Paul was referring to in this verse? If everything is permissible, then why not do it? Why would you choose to do things that are not beneficial to you? Is it sometimes a hard choice to fight against choosing things that are not beneficial to you? Do you think God understands that? Do you think that you need to master yourself and not let your hormones master you? Are you alone in this struggle?

Romans 1:25. What lies do you think the devil wants youth to believe? Is it that you are missing something in your life and sex is the thing you are missing? If you believe this lie, will you be exchanging the truth of God for something else? Is it easy to get hooked on this lie? What can you do if you are hooked on sex outside of the will of God? Can you be forgiven? Does God's grace extend to even sexual sins?

Song of Solomon 2:7. When does God want "love" to be awakened? What was His original plan? Why is God's plan best for us? What are some of the consequences of "waking love" before it should be? If you participate in sexual things outside of marriage and have to face the consequences, does that mean God doesn't love or forgive you?

Matthew 5:28. Is this the spiritual side of the commandment? How do you stop thinking lustfully? Does what you put into your mind (pictures, videos, talking with others) affect your thoughts and heart? Is lusting tied to masturbation?

Job 31:1. How did Job make a plan to keep free from sexual sin? Was this an impulsive thought or did it involve making a choice? Is this plan something you can do in your life? Can you do it on your own? Job made a choice, and you have a choice to make, too. God will help you make the right choice if you ask Him.

Philippians 4:8. How can the words in this verse help you overcome sexual sin? What things do you think about that need to be changed? What new things can you substitute for those things you should put out of your life? Will this take conscious thought and prayer to do? Is it worth the cost to change your habits?

God will help you! You are not alone. God treasures you with respect, dignity, and love. He wants you to value yourself that way, too!

EXTRA GEM

Ellen White was shown the struggles youth have with thoughts that can lead them away from their Father. Read what she writes: "Those who desire immortality must not allow an impure thought or act. If Christ be the theme of contemplation, the thoughts will be widely separated from every subject which will lead to impurity in action. The mind will be strengthened by dwelling upon elevating subjects. If trained to run in the channel of purity and holiness, it will become healthy and vigorous. If trained to dwell upon spiritual themes, it will come naturally to take that channel. But this attraction of the thoughts to heavenly things cannot be gained without the exercise of faith in God, and an earnest, humble reliance upon him for that strength and grace which will be sufficient for every emergency" (*Christian Temperance and Bible Hygiene,* p. 139).

Sharing Time

The Greek word for sexual immorality in Corinthians is the word *porneia.* Does that word look familiar? It's where we get the English word "pornography." Porneia isn't just something you look at, or watch; it can be pictures stored in your head. How can you help someone who has a problem with porneia? Tell them that sexual sin can be overcome just like any other sin. It takes prayer, and lots of it! Help them turn their thoughts to other things by not allowing a lot of idle time. Pray with them and then do something fun. Make sure they have good Christian fellowship to help them withstand the devil's temptations.

Consider This

Make a list of 10 things you can do when you are tempted by sexual sin. Include prayer on your list because it is one of your best weapons against the enemy. Make your list personal and use it to help you when times get rough.

Spirit of Prophecy
a real woman with a special gift

The intent of this study is to encourage young people to see that Ellen White, though a servant of the Lord and a true prophet, was also a very human and kind woman, who loved her family, had a sense of humor, and cared about others. In exploring who she was and what she wrote, it should help them want to know what the Bible says and want to read it even more.

Icebreaker
Getting to Know You

She's someone you never met but someone you should get to know. She was one of the most prolific authors ever. She wrote more than 25 million words during her lifetime. She is also the most translated of American authors. As with most writers, she was a prolific reader. Her personal library contained more than 1,000 volumes. She spent summers in the Colorado Rockies horseback riding, hiking, and relaxing. She was also a world traveler, and for her time that was unusual for a woman. She had a wonderful sense of humor and loved to use it. Her favorite hymn was "Peace Like a River," and she often requested it at church. Her favorite foods were corn soufflé, macaroni and tomatoes, and mustard greens. She loved people and animals. She had four sons, and they were the loves of her life. She cared about others who were hurting and often slipped them money when they were in need. She loved her family, her church, and her Lord.

You may know who she is, but you really should get to know who she was. You might be surprised at what you'll find out. Most see her as a stern prophet, but in fact, she was just an ordinary woman with feelings and desires much like you, doing what God had called her to do.

Ellen Gould Harmon White was born in Gorham, Maine. She also had a twin sister. They were the youngest of eight children in the family. Her parents and the family attended a Methodist Episcopal church. They were all devout Christians and loved the Lord. When they were 9, Ellen and her sister, Elizabeth, were walking home from school. And just as in today's society, there were bullies. This one was a 13-year-old that decided to pursue Ellen and her sister. The Harmon children had been taught to go home if someone was picking on them instead of fighting back. They were doing just that when Ellen turned to see how far the girl was behind them. As she turned, the bully threw a stone that hit Ellen in the nose. Not realizing how badly she had been hurt, she tried to continue on her way home but soon fainted. The devastation from this attack would stay with her the rest of her life. Because of the injury and its lingering effects, Ellen grew very sad, and as a result she turned to the Lord for comfort.

Dig In

Ellen was only 17 when she had her first of an estimated 2,000 visions given by God. She was a shy young woman, disfigured from her injury, and an unlikely choice to be a prophet. But God called to her and after some initial hesitation, she answered, agreeing to be His willing servant. Her visions and dreams, her writings, and her public speaking were all inspired by God's Spirit.

She wrote in the mid to late 1800s and continued up to her death in 1915. She witnessed countless world changes and catastrophes. She knew loss in her own life—losing one son as an infant, and another at age 16. Her life and writings have often come under scrutiny both in her day and today. Why did she open herself up to this kind of burden? Because she loved the Lord, and she loved others. She wanted all to know God's love. Sometimes, that simple desire can cause great heartache, as the devil tries to discredit your work. It did for Mrs. White. But the reward for her and all of God's servants will be out of this world.

Hot Potato

Prophet of Destiny or Fiction?

In recent years Ellen White has been called a plagiarist. She has been called a false prophet. Much has been done to discredit not only what she wrote but who she was as a person. Why? Could it be that her work has pointed others to the truth found in the Bible—something they are not ready or willing to admit?

In everything she wrote or spoke about, the Bible was her mainstay. She wrote what God shared to help others understand more closely what Scripture tried to teach. She never desired that her words would be put above those of Holy Scripture. She wanted humanity to study God's Word and hoped that her writings would lead others to fall in love with the character of God and desire Him more. And if you read her writings, you won't be able not to do that. You will find the character of God displayed in all its beauty and fall in love all over again.

Hot Potato Questions

- Some think that what Ellen White had to say was for another time. Do you feel that way or not? Why?
- Aren't scientists today proving what she has said about health issues and diet? Why is a prophet not only for their own time but for all time?
- What other prophets' works found in the Bible are we still using today? Does God give prophets words for their time that also can apply to the future?
- Why do you think God gives us prophets?
- What do you think it says about His character? Does the Bible tell us how to tell if a prophet is from the Lord?

Bible Discovery

Deuteronomy 18:21, 22; Jeremiah 28:9. What is the first test of a true prophet? What does God say will happen to the predictions that they make? What would cause a false prophet to be exposed for who they really are? Did the statements of Ellen White concerning her visions come true? Are we even discovering things about health today that make her writings valid? Do you feel that what Ellen White wrote long ago can impact your life today? What is to be our true source of light?

Isaiah 58:1; 1 Corinthians 14:3, 4. What are some of the reasons God gives prophets to His people? Part of a prophet's duty is to bring comfort to the church and to encourage us. Do you think this would be an easy part of the prophet's job? Another part of a prophet's job is to point out sin. Why might this be an unpleasant part of a prophet's job? Do you think it makes the life of a prophet easy or hard? How are most prophets treated? Did Ellen White want the job of a prophet? After her first vision she would not tell others about it until Hazen Foss visited her. He had been given a vision just before Ellen, but refused to be the Lord's messenger. Afterward, he came and told Ellen not to refuse the work of the Lord. Do you think it must have been overwhelming to a 17-year-old? Does she pass this test of a prophet: encouraging the church, giving comfort, edifying, and pointing out sin?

1 John 4:1-3; 2 Peter 1:20, 21. Is a prophet ever to give their own opinion? If not their opinion, what are they to tell others about? Who gives them what they are supposed to share? What defines Scripture? Is it Scripture that defines Scripture or humanity? Will a true prophet ever want publicity and fame? Whose glory does a prophet of God seek? What truth about Jesus will a true prophet teach? (Leaders, point out that a true prophet preaches the incarnation of Jesus, that He came to earth and took on the form of humanity so that He could redeem us.) Did Ellen White ever seek glory for herself? Did she ever try to put her will into her writings, or did she write what she was shown? Did she practice what she wrote?

Exodus 15:20; Judges 4:4; 2 Chronicles 34:22; Luke 2:36; Acts 21:8, 9. Does gender or age make a difference in whom God chooses as prophets? Why do you think this is? Do you think that Ellen White's weakness in physical strength as a result of her injury at age 9 made her better able to serve as a prophet? Why do you think that way? Can our weakness be God's strength? Have you ever experienced this in your life?

Matthew 7:15-20. What warning are we given about false prophets, especially for this age? Have there been false prophets in the past few years that appeared to be faithful, but their lives showed them to be "ferocious wolves" (NIV)? (Leaders, remind your group about false prophets such as David Koresh and Jim Jones and how they led their followers to their deaths. Your group is probably too young to remember them. Also, people such as Benny Hinn are alive today and have made predictions that have not been substantiated.)

What fruits will the lives of true prophets have? Did Ellen White bear good fruit with her life? Do you believe that Ellen White was a prophet of the Lord? Why or why not? Do you think her writings are still worthy of reading and studying? Does reading them make you want to read and understand the Bible more? If so, then is that exactly what she wanted to do with her life? Do you want to be a servant of God and let Him lead in your life?

EXTRA GEM

Read what Ellen White wrote about her own life and her calling:

"Early in my youth I was asked several times, Are you a prophet? I have ever responded, I am the Lord's messenger. I know that many have called me a prophet, but I have made no claim to this title. My Savior declared me to be His messenger. 'Your work,' He instructed me, 'is to bear

171

My word. Strange things will arise, and in your youth I set you apart to bear the message to the erring ones, to carry the word before unbelievers, and with pen and voice to reprove from the Word actions that are not right. Exhort from the Word. I will make My Word open to you. It shall not be as a strange language. In the true eloquence of simplicity, with voice and pen, the messages that I give shall be heard from one who has never learned in the schools. My Spirit and My power shall be with you.

"'Be not afraid of man, for My shield shall protect you. It is not you that speaketh: it is the Lord that giveth the messages of warning and reproof. Never deviate from the truth *under any circumstances*. Give the light I shall give you. The messages for these last days shall be written in books, and shall stand immortalized, to testify against those who have once rejoiced in the light, but who have been led to give it up because of the seductive influences of evil.'

"Why have I not claimed to be a prophet? Because in these days many who boldly claim that they are prophets are a reproach to the cause of Christ; and because my work includes much more than the word "prophet" signifies. When this work was first given me, I begged the Lord to lay the burden on someone else. The work was so large and broad and deep that I feared I could not do it. But by His Holy Spirit the Lord has enabled me to perform the work which He gave me to do" (*Selected Messages,* book 1, p. 32).

Sharing Time

Are the writings of Ellen White something you are comfortable sharing with others? Now that you have studied her life and the tests of a true prophet, maybe you are more open to her writings. Her book *Steps to Christ* is the most translated book in the world except the Bible. Pick up a few copies and share them with friends. Even those from other churches and religions will find little that they can object to in this book. It is a good place to begin your study of Mrs. White's writings.

Consider This

Many wonderful books and articles have been written about Ellen White, her ministry, and her life. Take some time this week to check out the following: *Stories of My Grandmother,* by Ella M. Robinson; *Meeting Ellen White,* by George Knight; *Ellen G. White: Prophet of Destiny,* by Rene Noorbergen, www.egwhite.com. There are many other good sites on the Internet. There are also those that claim she is a false prophet. Be sure of what you know and learn to choose wisely.

Spiritual Gifts

discover them—use them

Before presenting this study to a group, make sure you have read through the whole lesson, taking note of all the leaders' notes throughout it. Young people are just becoming aware of their gifts chosen by their heavenly Father just for them. Helping them see what they are good at can help them choose to use their talents for God.

Icebreaker
Small but Mighty

What can carry 10 to 20 times its own body weight, has the estimated brain processing power of a Macintosh II, and works in teams to pull off amazing feats? What has legs so swift compared to its body size that if they were compared to a human, it could run as fast as a horse? If you guessed the ant, then you are right! Ants may be small, but they are mighty!

Scientists have long studied ants. Their efficiency has been the model of many studies. And we can learn a few lessons from our six-legged friends.

The ant's brain is the largest of all the insect world. Believe it or not, scientists have proven that an ant's brain has 250,000 brain cells. (The average human brain has 10 billion.) And since ants live in huge colonies, an average colony of 40,000 would have about the same size brain as a human.

Scientists have also proved something else. By putting different-colored dots on the back of ants, they have been able to study and define their infrastructure. Ants have built-in instincts to perform jobs that help the whole colony. They use these natural talents to do some of the very things we humans do. Ants perform livestock farming, child care, education, climate control, have their own armed forces and security, do social planning, engineering, and practice communication skills. There are even worker ants that are assigned to garbage control. Their job is to keep everything neat and tidy. So they carry out the trash and place it in their very own garbage dump. Ants are so amazing at their engineering abilities that they can tunnel from two directions and still meet exactly in the middle! Ants have taught us a lot in their ability to work together as a team. They each have specific assigned duties, and they carry them out with speed and efficiency.

Think about all that the next time you're thinking of squashing those uninvited picnic guests!

Dig In

The Bible tells us that we should study the ant too. Look at Proverbs 6 and you will see that Solomon, too, found the tiny creatures fascinating. The Bible goes on to say that the church should act a little like an ant colony. Only it calls us (the church) a body instead of a colony. It tells us that we must work together for the common good of the whole church. It even defines skills and talents (called spiritual gifts) that each person is given in order help strengthen the body and keep the church running smoothly.

What are these gifts? They are found in Ephesians 4:11-13, Romans 12:4-9, and 1 Corinthians 12:7-11. Take the time to look these texts up and read them for yourself. You'll see the list includes things such as ministry, teaching, service, giving, leadership, mercy, helping, knowledge, and faith.

Some are tempted to say that they don't have any of these gifts. But we all have at least two. When we accept Christ as our Savior, we have the gift of faith. We can't believe in His saving grace without faith. Then the Holy Spirit comes into our lives and gifts us with at least one other gift to help us grow and for us to use to help others.

So how do you know what gift you have received? Here are a few ideas to get you started. First, look at what you are good at. Is it getting up in front of others—something that brings fear to many people? Then teaching and leadership may be your thing. Like to sing? Then music ministry is probably for you. If you stop and make a list, you'll probably see that you can easily identify at least one of your gifts. Another thought is to look at your passions. Not just the things you are good at, but those you have a real passion for. God puts these in our hearts for a reason. He created you, and He knows the desires of your heart. He gives us things He knows we will enjoy. That is a loving God! Pray! Don't forget that God has told us to ask. So ask Him what your gifts are and what He wants you to do with them. But listen, too. Because if you ask, He will answer. And while you are asking, talk with others around you: friends, family, teachers, church mates. They have watched you for some time, and they probably have a good idea of areas in which God has gifted you. Some of their answers may surprise you! (Leaders, you may want to take some time and talk within your group about the gifts that you think each person possesses. This will help the youth to get started on their own inventory.)

Hot Potato

Are you a sluggard? Did you read those verses in Proverbs 6:6-11? If not, do it now. The Bible says that the sluggard should study the ways of the ant. Are you a sluggard? What exactly is a sluggard? (Leaders, make sure you have a good definition for the word, but let the youth try to define it first.) In this instance, it seems to be a person that is held captive to leisure.

Hot Potato Questions

- In your life, how are you like an ant? How are you like a sluggard?
- Are you "held captive" to leisure—enjoying entertainment more than service? In what areas do you need to ask God for help in being faithful to the talents He has gifted you with?

Bible Discovery

Jeremiah 33:3. What does this verse tell us about being able to ask God the things that are on our hearts? Do you believe that He will tell you about your spiritual gifts if you ask Him? Have you tried? What would keep you from seeking God's guidance? Do you have any fears about what God might ask you to do? Do you think He would ask you to do something you might not enjoy?

1 Corinthians 12:4-6. Does everyone have the same gift? Why do you think that God gave different gifts to different people? Why do these verses remind us that each person has different gifts, but they are given by the same Spirit and the same Lord? Do people in your church ever forget that they are working on the same team? Do you?

Colossians 3:23, 24. How do these verses remind you of the work that ants do? Have you ever seen a lazy ant? How are we to use our talents and abilities? For our gain, or for others? Are we to do the things we are good at for people's applause? How do you feel when you are applauded by others? Do you give the glory to God?

1 Peter 4:10. Do you use your gifts to serve others or yourself? What does the Bible say about that? Is it wrong to enjoy your gifts? In what areas have you received grace from God? How can you use your gifts to let others know about the gift of grace that you have received?

Matthew 25:14-28. Why do you think that Jesus told this parable of the talents? Do you know that in today's monetary system a talent would have been roughly US$1,000? Were the servants who invested the money they were given treated differently? Were they each praised, not for what they had gained, but because they had proven they could be trusted? Do you think Jesus wants us to show that we can be trusted in the little things, so that He can give us more and more of His goodness?

EXTRA GEM

Ellen White loved to use her talents to encourage young people. Read what she says in *Messages to Young People,* page 39: "Your intellectual and moral faculties are God's gifts, talents entrusted to you for wise improvement, and you are not at liberty to let them lie dormant for want of proper cultivation, or be crippled and dwarfed by inaction. It is for you to determine whether or not the weighty responsibilities that rest upon you shall be faithfully met, whether or not your efforts shall be well directed and your best."

Sharing Time

Define at least one of your gifts. How can you use that gift this week to reach out to others who may not know God? Make a plan to use your gift this week—write something special, take food to somebody in need, help a friend see that they need to stop a destructive habit, forgive someone who won't expect it, tutor a fellow student who could use some help. Don't keep your gift to yourself—remember what happened to the unfaithful servant.

Consider This

Start an inventory of your spiritual gifts. Write them down. Pray about them. Ask others what they see as your strengths. Be open to trying something new that you haven't done before. You may be surprised that God has something in store for you that you never imagined!

Spiritualism
traditions, superstitions, New Age

Our young people today are getting caught up in things that they may not even be conscious of. This study touches on just a few of these. Let this study lead you and your young people to examine their lives and see if influences not from God are a part of their lives. And help them understand that with God they can overcome the unseen battle raging around them.

Icebreaker
The Danger of Tradition

Do you have triskaidekaphobia? Are you sure? You might want to get it checked out. After all, if you look at the calendar there will come a Friday the thirteenth. Triskaidekaphobia is the irrational fear of the number 13. And many people let this phobia guide their lives. Ever been to a high-rise hotel or hospital? Most don't have a thirteenth floor. So maybe the number 13 doesn't bother you. But it does bother a lot of people around the world. It's all part of a set of superstitions that you may not even be aware of. Most are rooted in ancient beliefs and practices, but the number 13 is actually based in the beginnings of Christianity. It was believed that there were 13 important guests at the Last Supper, the thirteenth being Judas. We all know what he did. His betrayal set into motion the death of Jesus on the cross. So, many people began to avoid the number 13. That practice has carried over through time and still affects our world. Many superstitions do affect your life. And before you start to deny it, let's look at some of the things we do and say and trace their origins.

The funny thing about superstition is that it has only the power we give to it. And most of us, without even being aware, give it some measure of power. Most superstitions came from ancient times when people that didn't understand nature and scientific principles tried to give an explanation to things they were ignorant on or feared. As scientific advances came about, many long-held superstitions were debunked. Since people used to not be able to explain why a seed produced vegetables, in ignorance they created an explanation that often involved things in the mystic world.

Ever crossed your fingers and made a wish? That's superstition at work. It was believed in times past that two lines that crossed could hold your wish in their center until your wish could come true. So people crossed their fingers and spoke their wish into them.

Ever heard that walking under a ladder would bring bad luck? That one is rooted in the Christian faith, too. People saw a ladder leaning against a wall as making a triangle with the ground. This was the symbol of the Trinity. If you violated that space you would be punished by a member of the Godhead. Sounds silly now, but do you avoid walking under a ladder?

Watch out, I'm going to sneeze. "Achoooo!" I know what you are going to say. Whatever language you might say it in, it all comes from the same ancient tradition. People used to believe that a person's spirit was found in their breath. If they sneezed, that breath could expel their very spirit or soul. If God's blessing was added, then the spirit wouldn't leave the body. Some cultures even blew back at the person, hoping to push the spirit back inside. You just had to hope that they weren't eating garlic at the time!

Dig In

So just how much of our culture is rooted in tradition and superstition? The answer is most of it. It is embedded in our lives. It is attached to much of what we do, and we practice it out of ignorance. That's one of the problems with tradition. Especially when it goes back for centuries. So what do we do?

Hot Potato

Practice Fear or Obey Love?

Much of what we do we do out of ignorance. But what happens when we actually fear these things? Do we keep practicing them, or turn to Jesus and obey Him out of love? In all of our cultures we are steeped in tradition. And while many traditions are based on families and values that are wholesome, some things we take for granted shouldn't be.

Young people today are especially vulnerable to practices and ways of life that take their focus away from God. Entertainment alone slips in practices and beliefs that, while very subtle, put them at risk. New Age thinking popularizes many things that in their very nature take us away from a God of love. Instead of a rigid set of rules, the appeal to New Age thinking is that you can pick and choose what suits you best. Among the most current trends is pantheism—the belief that God is all things and in all things, so in fact, the individual is a form of God. While we were created in His image, until He transforms us at His second coming, the Bible makes it plain that all have sinned and fallen short of the glory of God. We are definitely not God!

Another phenomenon that is transforming the world is the belief in angels. Yes, there are angels, both good and bad. But, as the master deceiver, the devil has again tried to take the focus off the One who created the angels and placed it on the angels themselves. The Bible tells us that God's angels have many purposes. They help us by providing physical needs, giving guidance, offering encouragement, and even rescuing us. They don't accept or desire worship. That belongs to God alone. The angels that fell with the devil love worship and love to masquerade as holy angels. They would love to work with you, but be aware—you will be working with demons. This current trend of angel culture all goes back to the devil's lie in the Garden of Eden—that we can become like God.

Hot Potato Questions
- Are there things that you do without thinking that can be traced back to superstition?
- Can you think of some of these?
- Is there any problem with practicing things that might have a deeper meaning if we don't intend that meaning? Why or why not?
- If you are made aware of the history of a tradition, and it is steeped in ancient ritual apart from God, should you keep practicing it?
- Why do you think the devil puts so much focus on tradition and superstition? What do you think he is trying to accomplish in us as a result?
- Are you aware of some of the new thinking, whether it is New Age thinking or the angel culture? Have you been caught up in any of it?
- Why is it so easy to follow a philosophy that allows you to pick and choose what to believe? Why would that be attractive to young people?
- What can you do to counter the influences that the media, entertainment, and technology have on your religious beliefs?

Bible Discovery
2 Corinthians 11:14. What does it mean to masquerade as an angel of light? Did you know that the devil can imitate things that can deceive us? Do you think his angels enjoy doing this, also? The angels that fell with the devil are the demons that the Bible speaks about. How

can we discern whether things are from God or not? What standard do we have to help us? How can we practice staying away from areas that might expose us to things that are not from God?

Deuteronomy 18:10-12. Why do you think God was so strict in His warning to the people not to practice these things? Did the nations around them do these evil things? Was God concerned that His people not be like those whose country they were entering? Is that part of why He wanted the children of Israel to drive the people completely out? Was practicing these things part of worshipping other gods? Was God jealous or was His jealousy righteous because He wanted us to love only Him for our benefit?

Ephesians 6:12. Whom are we in a war against? Is this something you think about? Is it easy to put it out of your mind since we don't always see the battle going on? Should we think more about this spiritual battle? Can we do anything to help us win this war? Can we do things that will help us lose the war? (Leaders, help your young people see that we can't do anything to win the war. It is only God and His power that can fight against the evil. But we can call on God and lean on Him to help us. We can rebuke the devil and his angels in God's name and power. We can also put ourselves in places and situations that will give us over to the power of evil by removing God's presence from us. In that way we are giving in to the enemy.) Can these beings that we battle against be real? Why do you think this way? Whose strength alone will help us and protect us?

Matthew 18:10; Psalm 91:11. Do you think we have guardian angels? Do you think that there can be things going on in the physical world that we live in and at the same time things going on in the spiritual realm that we need protection from? Do we always know when God's angels are ministering to us? Have you ever had an encounter with one of God's angels that you know of? What do you think when others share their angel encounters? Is this a source of encouragement or are we focusing too much on angels? Why do you feel this way?

John 14:6. Who is the source of truth for Christians? What ways does He use to help us learn the truth? (Leaders, mention the Bible as the number one way to know truth.) Can we let God show us the right things for us to do in our lives? Are you willing to change some of the things you do and believe in if they are found to be against God's desire for your life? What methods will you use to choose what is right in your life with God? Do you need to become more aware of the unseen battle going on around you? Don't forget, you can't do it by yourself. Only in Christ's strength can we be successful!

EXTRA GEM

Ellen White writes about guardian angels. Read what she wrote:
"Every redeemed one will understand the ministry of angels in his own life. The angel who was his guardian from his earliest moment; the angel who watched his steps, and covered his head in the day of peril; the angel who was with him in the valley of the shadow of death, who marked his resting place, who was the first to greet him in the resurrection morning—what will it be to hold converse with him, and to learn the history of divine interposition in the individual life, of heavenly cooperation in every work for humanity" (*Maranatha*, p. 314)!

Sharing Time

Most cultures are saturated now with this angel phenomenon. It is easy to think that angels are all good, but the truth is that a third of them—created holy—fell with the devil and sin. So how can you encourage others to see that not all angels are from God? Remind them that (1) God's angels never contradict the Bible, (2) God's angels will always be consistent with God's character, and (3) any encounter with an angel will glorify God, not the angel. Take a look at your own life and decide whether there are things you need to change that might be putting you on dangerous ground.

Consider This

Read Hebrews 13:2. How can we live our lives so that we can entertain angels without being aware of it? What things can we do that might minister to others? Make a list of things to do to share God's love and light with others in your daily life. How can you best witness in the things you do every day that can show the light of heaven to others?

Stewardship
time, talents, money

Leaders, when you mention stewardship to young people, one of two things usually happens: either they immediately tune you out or they think only of money. But stewardship goes far beyond our tithes and offerings. Helping your young people learn this lesson early will grow their relationship with God. Help them see that honoring God with their finances, their time, and their talents will reward them more than they can imagine! Don't be afraid to share your own testimony on how God has blessed you for honoring Him.

Icebreaker
A Day at the Beach

What do you do on a day at the beach? Soak in the sun, surf the waves, nap under your umbrella? Maybe you take a good book and a picnic and enjoy the day with your family. But there are others that take their time at the beach seriously. Very seriously.

They are professional sand sculptors. And they are found throughout the world. Their creativity and artistry are incredible. Sand scupture competitions are held all over the world. One of the most famous is the Harrison Hot Springs Sand Sculpture Contest held in British Columbia, Canada, since 1989. There the conditions are just right to build enormous and elaborate creations that usually last several months. The chosen designers submit their ideas to a committee, who then have preformed blocks of sand ready for the carvers. All entrants start carving from the top down and work three eight-hour days to finish their designs. (Leaders, look up photos on the Internet of some of these competitions to share with your youth. The variety and designs are awesome.)

The history of sand-castle building dates back throughout time and is thought to have been an early form of communication. It is also thought that the ancient Egyptians used sand castles as models before constructing the pyramids. About 100 years ago on the New Jersey (U.S.A.) coast, a man named James Taylor started building sand sculptures at the beach and asked for donations from his viewers.

Taylor made about 50 cents a week, which wasn't too bad for his day. It is thought that modern sand-sculpting started there, and it is now a sunny competition all over the world.

There is just something so inviting about playing in the sand. There is also something dangerous about it.

Dig In

The Bible talks about building houses in the sand. In Matthew 7:24-27 we read what Jesus says about the foolish building their house upon the sand. Remember what He says will happen? It all ends in a crash. A big one!

In that same passage we are told that the wise build their houses on the rock. Only it should be spelled the Rock, because Jesus told us that if we listen to His words and put them into practice we will be considered wise.

Hot Potato

I Will Versus Thy Will

God has called us to be wise stewards. That means we are managers with responsibilities and obligations. A steward takes care of someone else's things. Joseph acted as Pharaoh's steward. His faithfulness to God and to what he was entrusted with helped to save a country during a famine.

What are we to be stewards of? Think for a moment. What do you have that is really yours? Who gave you the things you have—and not just material things—but things such as time, health, abilities? Do you think the answer is God? Do you agree that everything we own, everything we are, is a gift from a loving Creator? Why or why not?

If everything belongs to God, how much of what we have are we to give back to Him? Don't be too quick to say 10 percent. That may seem like the logical answer, since we all know that God has called us to give our tithe to Him. But hasn't He also asked us for 14 percent of our time (the Sabbath)?

Hot Potato Questions

- If we faithfully give our tithe and keep the Sabbath as God asks, have we met our obligation to Him?
- What can you give to someone who gives you everything?

- How does the fact that God made you His steward affect your decisions?
- Does God need what you have to give?

Bible Discovery

Ephesians 5:16, 17. This verse warns us that the times are evil. How do you think that these verses, written almost 2,000 years ago, apply to today? Are there more things we need to consider today that can make us "unwise" than there were at the time these verses were written? How can you personally live more wisely? How do these verses affect you as a steward?

Colossians 3:23, 24. As a steward, whom are you working for? Will you get your pay on this earth? Why or why not? Are you still willing to work as a good steward if you have to wait for your reward? How does being a good steward of your time, money, and talents benefit you? How does it benefit others? (See also Matthew 6:19, 20.)

Luke 16:10-13. How does God build trust in us? Have you felt this happening in your life? Why do you think that we cannot serve two masters? What difficulties might you encounter if you tried? Can you be a good steward for the Lord and still let worldly things distract you from His will?

1 Timothy 6:10. Is the love of money the root of all evil? Have you ever heard this verse misquoted? Does God want us to use our money only for His cause? Is wanting to gain wealth wrong? How can the pursuit of money and fame cause someone to wander from the faith? What do you think this verse means when it says that those who have wandered have "pierced themselves with many griefs" (NIV)? (Read also verses 17-19 from this chapter.)

2 Corinthians 9:6, 7. What do you think the Bible means when it says that "God loves a cheerful giver" (NIV)? Can you give without being happy about it? Would that fulfill an obligation to God? Why do you think God wants us to give Him our time, talents, and money? In what specific ways can you be more generous in giving God your time, talent, and money?

Matthew 25:14-30. This is the parable of the talents. A talent in today's currency would be about $1,000. Did all of the servants receive the same amount? But were each given something? Was their reward based on the amount given? Did all the servants receive praise? Why not? Is it the amount that we are entrusted with (whether time, money, or talents) or what we do with them that counts? How would you stack up in this parable?

EXTRA GEM

Ellen White understood that God gives us everything. She was shown by our loving Father that we need to understand this, even as youth. Read what she wrote:

"The youth need to understand the deep truth underlying the Bible statement that with God 'is the fountain of life.' Not only is He the origi-nator of all, but He is the life of everything that lives. It is His life that we receive in the sunshine, in the pure, sweet air, in the food which builds up our bodies and sustains our strength. It is by His life that we exist, hour by hour, moment by moment. Except as perverted by sin, all His gifts tend to life, to health and joy" (*The Faith I Live By,* p. 164).

Sharing Time

Stewardship is a biblical principle that we have to put into action. God wants us to give so that He can give back. If we fail to give back to Him, we are robbing Him of the chance to pour out His blessings on us, and oh how He wants to do that! Think of ways that you have been faithful in giving. What blessing did you receive as a result? Think of someone in your life that would benefit from learning about this blessing. Pray and ask God whom you can share that blessing with this week.

Consider This

Make an inventory of the things most precious to you—your top 10 list. Make sure you include the talents that you enjoy the most. Look close-ly at the list and decide which areas you are being a wise steward in. Are there other areas in which you need to improve your stewardship? In what ways can you do this?

Substance Abuse

clear minds, pure hearts

B e prepared when using this study in a group setting. Many youth will have strong feelings about the subject, and others will not want to be open about their knowledge or use of the substances. Make sure you are covered in prayer as you present this important study to your young people.

Icebreaker

You Can't Tickle Yourself!

Did you know that tickling has been the subject of many studies for several years? Great minds such as Plato, Bacon, and Galileo studied it extensively. Scientists have been fascinated with the responses for years.

The response to tickling is a strange one. It involves both pleasure, pain, and something else: the element of surprise. That's why scientists hypothesize that people cannot tickle themselves. The part of your brain involved in the tickle response is the cerebellum, or "little brain." It is here that responses to sensory sensations are processed, and it distinguishes whether sensory information is expected or not. But to be tickled, most people must be surprised.

But did you know that there are some people that can be tickled without being touched? Just the anticipation that they are going to be tickled produces a response—usually a giggle—before they are even touched!

All of these responses come from one of the most amazing parts of our bodies: the brain. Our bodies are certainly complex, but the brain seems to be the crowning jewel of the body. On average, it weighs just three pounds, but it uses 20 percent of the oxygen you breathe and 20 percent of the blood your body circulates! In fact, the brain has more than 100,000 miles of blood vessels. If you could take them out and lay them straight, they would circle the earth more than four times! For such a small organ, it certainly is complex!

The brain needs lots of blood circulation and air because of the 100 billion neurons that constantly process everything in and around you. The neurons are responsible for processing each sensation, thought, and action the body produces.

Dig In

The brain is an amazing organ. But unfortunately, many teens choose to harm theirs. How and why? you may ask.

They do it by abusing substances that work on the brain, such as drugs, nicotine, and alcohol. Drugs work on the limbic system in the brain, which is the "reward" system in our bodies. The limbic system responds to pleasure by releasing a substance called dopamine, which helps to create feelings of pleasure. Since we need natural pleasures in our lives to survive, the limbic system drives us to seek these things. The first time a person uses harmful drugs, the body responds by flooding itself with dopamine. The brain immediately changes as a result of this flood, and dopamine receptors in the brain are reduced. After a while the limbic system craves the drug, and a vicious cycle begins, taking up more and more dopamine to feel normal again.

The body's response to alcohol is similar, as the 3 million teens who suffer from alcoholism can affirm. Millions more have unmanageable drinking problems. It's especially sad when you realize that alcohol is a major factor in the three leading causes of death among teens: auto accidents, murders, and suicides. Scientists have proven that youth who drink before the age of 15 are four times more likely to develop dependence on alcohol than those who start after the age of 21.

Why would teens use drugs and alcohol? You answer that one. Why are youth tempted to use substances that abuse their bodies? (Leaders, be prepared to provide some answers to prompt the youth. Try to give everyone a chance to respond.)

It all comes back to abusing that marvelous organ God designed— your brain!

Hot Potato

The Latest Trend

Teens today haven't had to look far for drugs. They have been getting them right at home in the medicine cabinet. Prescription medicine abuse has risen in alarming rates among teens. Most teens think that prescription meds are safe because they are legitimate. They think that they are not as dangerous or addictive as street narcotics. Because they are more readily available and easier to use compared to other street narcotics, there is a perception of safety. These drugs work differently on the bodies of healthy people than on those for whom the medications were prescribed, and they are very addictive and extremely dangerous! Yet it is estimated that 20 percent of teens have abused prescription meds or cough medications.

Hot Potato Questions

- "Everyone is doing it!" Have you heard that from your friends?
- Have you ever been tempted to try something?
- What advice can you give to help others when they are pressured to "just try it"?

Bible Discovery

1 Corinthians 10:13. Does this verse tell you that you will never be tempted? Why do you think God permits us to be under temptation? Do you face temptation from your peers as a result of alcohol and drug abuse? What can you say or do when confronted with these temptations? How can you help others understand that they can be strong when faced with these potentially deadly substances? Is temptation itself a sin?

1 Corinthians 6:20. Do you consider your body a temple of God? In what ways do you do this? This verse speaks about a price—with what price are you purchased? How should that affect the way you treat your body?

1 Peter 5:8; Titus 2:11-14. What do these verses tell us we should practice? How do you define self-control? Does practicing self-control give us the strength to resist evil? With whose power can you "just say no"? Have you ever had to practice saying no to these kinds of temptations? Were you successful? Why or why not?

Romans 13:13; 1 Thessalonians 5:7, 8. What do you think living "in the daytime" means? Why are we encouraged not to live in the dark? Does the cover of darkness hide the bad things we do from God? Why do we belong to the day? Can people hide their abuse of alcohol and drugs? Can you help someone who is trying to hide their abuse of these substances? What can you do?

1 Corinthians 10:31-11:1. What do these verses tell us we should be for others? Can seeing you set a good example help someone else overcome an addiction? Why or why not? What is the best way to be a good example? Should you always use words? Did Jesus give us an example to follow when He was here on the earth? What is the best way to be connected to Him so that we can follow His example and help others?

1 Peter 2:16; 2 Peter 2:17-20. If you are free in Christ, why should you choose to live a healthy lifestyle and not use substances such as alcohol, nicotine, and drugs? How do people use their freedom to cover their habits? Have you seen examples of this? Do people who push drug use promise freedom and pleasure? Can they offer these things? Who alone can offer you true freedom from all temptations? (Hint: see John 8:36.)

EXTRA GEM

Do you think that substance abuse is new to your generation? Apparently not. Ellen White was shown what such abuses brought on the youth of her day:

"On every side Satan seeks to entice the youth into the path of perdition; and if he can once get their feet set in the way, he hurries them on in their downward course, leading them from one dissipation to another, until his victims lose their tenderness of conscience and have no more the fear of God before their eyes. They exercise less and less self-restraint. They become addicted to the use of wine and alcohol, tobacco and opium, and go from one stage of debasement to another. They are slaves to appetite. Counsel which they once respected, they learn to despise" (*Mind, Character, and Personality,* vol. 1, p. 76).

Sharing Time

Some of your friends might argue that smoking pot is natural; after all, God gave humanity every plant in the beginning, right? (See Genesis 1:29, 30.) He gave the grasses to the beasts of the earth as food. It is mankind who is using things in ways that God never intended. Share with your friends that Adam and Eve let the devil trick them into thinking the same lie, and look what it cost them. Tell them not to let the devil whisper the same lie into their ear and be fooled. The price is just too high to get high!

Consider This

Abusing alcohol and drugs can do many things to your mind. One of them is to dull your senses and cause impaired judgment.

When your judgment is impaired, things such as sexual assault and unprotected sex can change your life forever. You are far too smart and have too much going for you to ruin it all. Don't make yourself vulnerable. Study the effects of drinking so that you can share them with others who need someone to stand with them against using harmful substances.

Suffering and Poverty
it's closer than you think

Much of the world lives in poverty and suffering. Help your young people realize God's grace in their lives and how they have an obligation to help others.

Icebreaker

In 1620 a colony of people left Europe in search of religious freedom. They landed in what was then called the New World (now known as the United States). They hoped to establish a place where people could worship as they chose. What they met in this new land were harsh conditions that they were unprepared for. A "great sickness" ran through the colony of Pilgrims that first winter of 1620, reducing the original number of settlers and crew by half. Persevering, the Pilgrims that remained were helped by local Native Americans. They learned to plant crops appropriate for the harsh New England weather. Summer passed and the time for gathering was upon them, and for the Colonists and the Indians the harvest meant giving thanks. For three days in 1621 the Pilgrims and the local Wampanoag Indians celebrated together. They dined on wild fowl and venison. The feast may have included things such as hasty pudding, fish, Indian corn, fry bread, and for dessert, wild plums and dried berries. And no, there probably wasn't any pumpkin pie. There were games of skill and strength, too. The feasting and fun brought the two groups closer and produced a peace that lasted 50 years.

Dig In

Many other countries around the world celebrate a time of thanksgiving. In Canada Thanksgiving is celebrated on the second Monday in October. In Malaysia and Singapore there is a celebration in mid-September to give thanks for the abundant summer harvest. During this celebration a mooncake is served. It is made of a sweet bean-paste filling with golden brown flaky skin. Family members gather to eat mooncake and admire the harvest moon together. In Brazil a special day of thanksgiving and prayer has been designated for the fourth Thursday of November, a tradition that began in 1949. Thanksgiving-like festivities occur in almost every culture. And the calorie count for a traditional thanksgiving dinner? Well, that runs between 2,500 and 4,000 calories!

Unfortunately, as we gather together around the world to eat, give thanks, and scrape our leftovers into the garbage, 963 million people in the world go hungry. Half of the world's population lives on less than US$2 a day. The majority of these people are women and children.

Hot Potato

We've all heard how we should finish our food because of the starving people in Africa. The truth is that the largest group of starving people live in the Asia Pacific region. There, more than 565 million people don't have enough to eat on a daily basis. And in case you think all starving people live beyond the United States border, guess again. The fact is that 21 percent of all children in the United States live in poverty, and unfortunately, statistics say that race is a factor. Forty-six percent of all African-American children and 40 percent of all Latino children live in poverty in the United States.

So what is poverty? One definition says it is the lack of goods and services commonly taken for granted by members of the mainstream society. Can poverty affect you? It certainly can. Almost 39 percent of Americans will live below the poverty line at some point in their life. Think about that the next time you scrape those plates into the garbage disposal.

Hot Potato Questions

- Have you done anything specific to help others who are in need? Be specific. What was your motivation?
- How do you think God feels about suffering and poverty in our world?
- Why do you think He allows human suffering and poverty?
- Have you ever had a time in your life that you were in need? How did that make you feel?
- As a Christian, are we held accountable for helping others who are in need?
- Is it your desire to want to help others more? Why or why not?
- What specific things could you do to help others who are in need?
- Do you always need money to help others? Why or why not?

Bible Discovery

Proverbs 22:2. Does God make a distinction between the rich and the poor? Since God loves all people, does how we treat others reflect on how we treat God? If we make distinctions and have no concern for those who are in poverty and have different needs, what is that saying to God?

Proverbs 14:31. Do we have a choice in how we treat the less fortunate if we are truly walking with God? Can you name some of the ways the poor might be oppressed? What would you feel like if you were in their place? How do you think others feel when we are kind and help them? Which way is the best way to show God's character to others, with oppression or mercy? Why do you feel that way?

James 1:27. God loves widows and orphans. Throughout Scripture His love and care of the less fortunate is evident. Why do you think God has a special place in His heart for those who are alone? Why would He tell us to make special provisions for those who are in need?

Are God's promises to the less fortunate conditional? Why or why not? What can you do personally to help others who are alone? Do they need more than food?

Luke 6:37, 38. What promise are we given in these verses? If we give generously of our time, money, and talents to help others, how will we be rewarded? Is it easy to see others in need and think that we are superior? Why do you feel that way? Does God want us to judge others, especially because of their situation? Do we sometimes put ourselves in bad situations by our own choice? Can we blame God if we aren't making the best choices for our lives? Do people do it anyway? How can we best show the character of God to others?

Psalm 37:25. What a promise! If someone is suffering from poverty and loss, can they trust that God will help them? This is a promise especially for His children. Can you claim this promise for yourself if times get tough? How can you know for sure that God will take care of you? (See verses 26-28.)

Revelation 21:3-5. Isn't it wonderful to know that someday soon all the poverty and suffering in this world will be over! Who will wipe all tears from our eyes? Can you imagine a world without suffering and poverty? What do you think it will feel like to those who have struggled all their lives just to find food to sustain life? Is the promise of a perfect world to come something that can help us if we are going through rough times? Verse 5 finds John being instructed to write the words down because they are "trustworthy and true" (NIV). Isn't that a wonderful footnote from God?

EXTRA GEM

Ellen White was shown that giving what we have to God for His use is the best way to live:

"The sower multiplies his seed by casting it away. So it is with those who are faithful in distributing God's gifts. By imparting they increase their blessings. 'Give, and it shall be given unto you,' God has promised; 'good measure, pressed down, and shaken together, and running over, shall men give into your bosom.' Luke 6:38" (*The Acts of the Apostles*, p. 345).

Sharing Time

What needs do you see in your community among the poor and suffering? What ways can you help? Make a list of at least two or three things you and your friends can do to help others, and then make it a point to work on achieving these goals. Start simple with activities such as collecting blankets for the homeless, and see where God leads you. Small steps add up to larger solutions.

Consider This

Look up "widows and orphans" in your Bible. See how many times we are given the challenge to take care of them. Write down your favorites of these verses and print them on index cards and memorize them. Then let the Word that is in you come out in service toward others.

Suicide

our lives are not our own

This is a difficult subject to discuss with young people, yet discussion is one of the best ways to prevent suicide. Open communication can help heal those affected by suicide. Pray for your young people.

Icebreaker

Have you ever heard the expression "the straw that broke the camel's back"? Sure you have, and you've probably felt that you've been there at least once. This is known as an idiom in English. It probably originated from an Arab proverb in which a camel was loaded with so much straw to transport that it impeded its capacity to move. Do you really think one piece of straw can make a difference? Check out the straw theory in other languages:

Danish—The drop that made the glass overflow
Dutch—The drop that makes the bucket overflow
French—The drop of water that makes the vase overflow
German—The drop that makes the barrel overflow
Spanish—The last drop that overflows the glass
Romanian—The drop that filled the glass

One of the earliest recordings of this metaphor dates back to 1655, when Anglican theologian J. Bramhall used a variation of this saying in an early work. The point is: there comes a breaking point for everyone, a moment when seemingly inconsequential additions can cause great breakdowns.

Think back to a time that you may have felt this way—that if one more thing happened you were just going to lose it. How did you feel in this situation? Stressed? Overwhelmed? Anxious? Depressed? Those can be normal responses to great stress, but it's what you do with them that matters. How did you get past this seemingly insurmountable roadblock?

Dig In

The Bible tells us that there are ways to hang on when the stresses of this life seem to overtake us. But many young people (and older ones, too) don't turn to God as their source of help in troubled times.

Hot Potato

They turn to suicide.

Suicide is now the third leading cause of death among young people worldwide. Other big causes are accidents, cancer, and AIDS. Yet suicide is preventable. Some people forget that suicide is a permanent solution to a temporary problem.

There are many keys that can trigger suicidal thoughts, and most youth admit that they have had these thoughts at times. If these thoughts have occurred to you, you're normal. But it's what you do when these thoughts occur that matters most.

Depression Quiz: Depression ranks as one of the leading causes of suicide among youth your age. Things such as parents divorcing, breaking up with a girlfriend/boyfriend, death of a relative or friend, problems at school, feelings of rejection, can all cause intense feelings that may be hard to handle. Signs of depression can follow. But how do you know if you are really depressed?

Look at the following questions and circle your answer to them. Think about the last couple weeks and how you have felt when answering them.

1. The future for me seems . . .
    A. Great—I can't wait for it.
    B. A struggle, but I'm doing OK
    C. I'm . . . well . . . pretty hopeless.

2. I'm finding it harder to concentrate.
    A. Not really!
    B. Just because I'm distracted.
    C. Yes. How did you know?

3. Making decisions is . . .
    A. The same as any other time.
    B. No fun, but I can make them.
    C. Harder than usual. I wish I had help.

4. Things that have always been fun . . .
    A. Are still fun.
    B. Fun when I have the time.
    C. Not so fun right now.

5. Lately . . . I feel more tired.
   A. Not really. I've got lots of get-up-and-go.
   B. Maybe a little, but I'm working hard.
   C. Yes, I could sleep all the time.

6. I spend time thinking about . . .
   A. How much fun life is.
   B. How much work I have to do.
   C. Ways . . . well . . . that I could check out of life.

7. Lately . . . I've lost or gained weight.
   A. Nope, still the same.
   B. A little, but who doesn't?
   C. Yes, without trying to diet.

If your answers are mostly A's, you are doing great! Keep up the good work.

If your answers are mostly B's, you're doing fine, too. There's always room for improvement.

If your answers are mostly C's, you may be experiencing some depression. There are many things that can cause depression. If you still feel this way in a week or two, though, reach out to someone you trust. Talking about it is one of the very best things you can do. If you can't speak with a parent or other relative, remember that you have others who care, too. Talk with your youth leader or a close friend. Don't just try to bury it.

Hot Potato Questions
- Do you think suicide is murder?
- Do you think a person committing suicide has a chance of going to heaven? Why do you feel this way?

Bible Discovery
Genesis 2:7. Is God the Creator and Sustainer of all life, including yours? Take a look at what the Bible says. If God is the Author of life, who has the right to decide when life should end? Do we ever have the right to choose life or death? Why or why not?

Isaiah 40:28. Does God ever grow weary? Can you trust Him when you are tired? How about when you are having thoughts of suicide, can you trust God to talk about them with Him? Do you think God understands you?

Psalm 46 and Psalm 121. Is the state of our world causing you to worry? Do your worries make you feel anxious or depressed? Where can you turn when you feel this way? David often felt exactly the way you do, that the world was upside down and that everyone had turned against him. So what did he do when he felt the weight of the world on his shoulders? Where did he turn? Can you do the same thing David did—turn to the Lord?

Matthew 14:27-32. The disciples were on the sea, and the wind was whipping the waves so much that these brave seamen feared for their lives. They saw someone walking toward them, and Peter realized it was Jesus. Jesus invited Peter to join Him on the water, and Peter did, but as soon as he took his eyes off the Lord, he began to sink. What happens to us when we take our eyes off the Lord? Do we sink into our problems? What can we do if we feel overwhelmed? What can you say to others who feel they can't handle their problems?

Genesis 18:25. Abraham was pleading with the Lord for Sodom—a city of great sin. He knew that his nephew Lot and his family were there and he wanted them spared from what was coming. Abraham was bold with God. Can you be bold with God, too? It takes faith, and Abraham knew that God was faithful and that He would judge fairly. Can you trust God as Abraham did to judge fairly?

EXTRA GEM

Ellen White writes the following in *Messages to Young People*, page 63:

"He [Satan] seeks to make the pathway as sorrowful as possible; but if you keep looking up, not down at your difficulties, you will not faint in the way, you will soon see Jesus reaching His hand to help you, and you will only have to give Him your hand in simple confidence, and let Him lead you. As you become trustful, you will become hopeful."

Sharing Time

Psalm 34:18, 19. These are wonderful verses to share with your friends who are hurting. Perhaps they need to be comforted. Suicide can be prevented with open communication and someone to talk to, someone who cares and who can be trusted. Will you be that friend for someone you know who is feeling that they are on their last straw? It sometimes takes only one person to reach out to help someone who is hurting.

Consider This

Look up Judges 16:26-31 and review the death of Samson. Do you think what he did should be counted as suicide? Why or why not? Did he want to kill himself or the Philistines? Is suicide ever justified?

Surviving School
a teachable heart

Leaders, it is important to remember that young people don't always have control over where they go to school. Your job is to be supportive of them, not judgmental. If they are in a situation in which they attend public school, they have numerous chances to witness. Supporting them can give them the strength to make good choices and trust God to lead them, something they will need very much.

Icebreaker
A Remarkable Journey

It weighs only half a gram (.018 ounces), yet it can fly with bursts of speed up to 22 miles per hour (35 kilometers). Each year the young make a trip they have never made before, yet manage to fly to their destination up to 2,000 miles (3,200 kilometers) away. What is this amazing creature? The monarch butterfly.

The black-and-orange beauty with its wingspan of three to four inches is one of the most widely recognized species of butterflies in the world. Early English settlers to the U.S. named the butterfly after their monarch, Wilhelm of Orange. Depending on their summer location, the butterflies migrate to different areas in the fall. The migration destination of the ones from eastern Canada and the eastern U.S. had long been a secret. But in 1976 their hiding place was finally found. Just northwest of Mexico's capital in a forest in the Sierra Madres, up to 100 million of the winged beauties winter on the trunks and branches of the fir trees. It is an amazing site that attracts many visitors to the area.

This high peak in Mexico provides the right environment for the butterflies to rest. It is cold and allows them to rest while using few calories during their winter siesta. But when spring arrives, they take lots of sunbaths to warm their flight systems and continue the long drive back to their summer grounds. Most of the original butterflies don't survive the journey north, but their offspring do.

Illegal cutting of the trees in this Mexican forest may lead to the extinction of an entire race of these beautiful butterflies. This deforestation may end one of the most amazing journeys ever.

Dig In

Did you know that you, too, are on an amazing journey? One that started when you were about 5 or 6. It won't end the way you think—upon high school graduation. No, the journey of your education should last long into your life and continue even more as we search the vast reaches of God's heavenly kingdom.

As a Christian young person, your education really begins at home. Your parents were given the job of educating you in the ways of your heavenly Father. They taught you about His love, His sacrifice for you, and that He would always be there to guide you as you go through life. With this knowledge both in your heart and in your head, you are equipped to go into the world and live and serve your heavenly Father.

Your parents also had the difficult job of deciding where you would receive your education. Perhaps they had some choices, depending on where you live and their income. They may have had the choice to send you to a school run by our church or to homeschool you. Others may not have had an option to send you anywhere but to public school.

Whatever the type of school you are in, there are challenges to be met, both by you and your parents. God has promised that He will be with you and give you the strength and grace to meet these challenges and excel.

Hot Potato
Whose Perspective?

So what do you do if you find yourself in public school? How do you handle the challenges presented in all areas of your life: your spirituality, your education, your lifestyle? The most important thing to know is that you don't need to do it by yourself. You have parents who love you. Their involvement with your school is the single most important aspect of your success. Whether you are in private school or public school, studies prove that parental involvement is what determines success. So don't be shy about having your parents around and poking into your school life. You need them.

School is all about choices no matter where you go. You have to make wise choices of friends, for they will influence you and you will influence them. Learn to be the one to give the wisest influence. If you do, others will follow. Sixteen percent of your time is spent in school after all. Making smart choices will help that time be used for your best.

Wherever you go to school, don't be afraid to make a stand for what you believe in. It may not be easy, but God never said it would be easy for any of us to choose to follow His ways. This is a world full of sin. Going against the tide is never easy, but the rewards will be out of this world. So stand up and proclaim the truth; there are others that need to hear what you have to say. Peer pressure is hard to deal with. Through prayer you can find the strength you need for every situation.

Hot Potato Questions

- Do you think there is more peer pressure in public school or church school? Why or why not?
- Do you think, if the choice were possible, that all Adventist youth should attend our private schools? Why or why not?
- What school situation are you in? Did you have a choice in your educational institution?
- Would you change school settings if you could? Why or why not?
- What challenges may be unique to attending public school? What ways can you think of to handle these challenges?

Bible Discovery

Proverbs 22:6. Is this a promise or a command? Who is it intended for, you or your parents? Can you learn any wisdom from this verse that will help you in your education? What does this verse tell you about the importance of training beginning in the home?

Proverbs 19:27. What teaching do you think Solomon was talking about in this verse? Where did Solomon's great wisdom come from? Can you, too, ask God for wisdom both in your education and how you approach the peer pressure you will inevitably encounter? Why do the things we encounter pull us away from God? Do they have to? Can you learn in an environment that doesn't always promote Christian ethics?

Psalm 32:8-10. Where can you turn when you need help in knowing what you are supposed to do regarding your education? Is this a promise you can depend on? Are you teachable? Being teachable means you are willing to listen and learn. Some people are smart and rely on their own strength, but the wisest ones are teachable. Do you believe God wants you to be teachable? Does that mean that you are weak or that you are strong? Have you ever met a stubborn mule or been like a stubborn mule? It's not easy to learn that way, is it?

Philippians 4:4-7. Do you have to be overpowering to speak the truth? Will people listen to you better if you have a gentle spirit? What opportunities do you have to witness at your school? Is it only with words or can you witness by your choices of lifestyle, clothing, food, or personality? If you are in public school, do you need to waste time fearing your setting? Why or why not? These verses mention prayer and petition, but they also mention thanksgiving as a source of peace. Why is thanksgiving (thankfulness and praise) an important part of seeking God and receiving His grace? What do these verses mention as one of the most important ways to live in God's peace? How can you guard your heart and mind wherever you are?

EXTRA GEM

Ellen White understood the importance of the home as the early and continued education ground for all youth. See what she writes: "The work of parents underlies every other. Society is composed of families, and is what the heads of families make it. Out of the heart are 'the issues of life' (Proverbs 4:23); and the heart of the community, of the church, and of the nation is the household. The well-being of society, the success of the church, the prosperity of the nation, depend upon home influences" (*The Ministry of Healing*, p. 349).

Sharing Time
Make a list of the ways that you are especially challenged in regard to your faith in the school setting. Pray about this list, seeking God's wisdom on how you can be most effective in sharing your convictions with others. Choose one area and try to make an effort this week to be a positive influence on others—whether it is your fellow students or perhaps a teacher.

Consider This
Talk with your family about their educational experiences. See how different or alike your experiences are. Really listen as they talk and see what you can learn from them about how to respond to God in all aspects of your education. Remember to be teachable!

Tattooing, Piercing, and Fashion

what are we expressing?

Leaders, this lesson's theme is learning about self-expression. Believe it or not, each of us expressed ourselves in some way when we were young. Was it platform shoes, bell bottoms, or some wild hairstyle for you? Young people today have more choices and more pressures to conform to others. Gently lead them to God's desire for them.

Icebreaker

Germs Can Kill!

They are so small, you'll likely never see them. But with a powerful microscope you'll spot the little rascals. They may be tiny, but they are mighty! Germs—the infamous invisible killers. In fact, germs and bacteria are the second leading cause of death in the United States. In fact, up to 17 percent of all deaths are blamed on the nasty little creatures.

Did you know that germs killed an American president? Yep, back in 1881 President Garfield was at the train depot catching a ride to the New Jersey seashore for a vacation, when Charles J. Guiteau came out of the shadows and shot the president twice. But it wasn't the bullets that killed the president. Doctors at the scene tried to remove the bullet with a metal instrument right at the train depot. When that wasn't successful, one of the doctors used his unwashed hands to probe for the bullet. What started as a three-inch wound became a 20-inch-long gash filled with germs. Guiteau might have thought he killed the president, but it was actually the doctors who finished the job.

According to the Centers for Disease Control and Prevention, it is estimated that there are 2 million hospital-acquired infections in the United States, leading to 90,000 deaths each year. The main culprit? Unwashed hands.

President Garfield's killers are still around today.

Some have tried to tackle the problem. Take King Henry IV. It was the king's command that his knights be clean. Well, at least once in their lives. He ordered them to bathe during their knighthood ceremony. That was it—just the one time.

Today, with all our knowledge of cleanliness, you always wash your hands, right? Women actually wash more than men. But do you know about the dirtiest objects around? You probably have one with you right now: your cell phone. Mobile phones have been proven to be one of the objects you handle that carry the most germs. Think about that the next time you text.

Dig In

All this talk about germs does have a point, besides reminding you to wash your hands. Some other behaviors that young people practice are just as dangerous as unwashed hands—both in their physical lives and in their spiritual ones.

God's Word talks about our body as the temple of God. So it would stand to reason that what we do to our bodies is important to God. Where do things such as tattooing, body piercing, and fashion fit into that? Is it important to your heavenly Father? The Bible says it is.

Yet people that don't follow the Bible think that tattooing and piercing are a great form of self-expression. Take Lucky Diamond Rich, who has spent more than 1,000 hours having his body modified by hundreds of tattoo artists. How much of his body? All of it—100 percent of his skin is covered in tattoos, and he is even getting them multilayered. Then there is Robert Jesus Rubio, who lives in Texas. In 2008 he had more than 900 piercings done with surgical needles.

What about fashion choices? Young people are expressing themselves well, thanks to the clothing manufacturers. Much of today's choices for you include things that are either offensive in wording, too sexy, too sloppy, or expressive of the gloomy side. Think about it the next time you look in the mirror. What are you trying to express?

What makes young people want to follow these practices? Most say it is a form of self-expression. But if you look at the people teens hold up as their "heroes," it's easy to see that the apple doesn't fall far from the tree. While most claim it's their idea of expressing themselves, it usually is owing to following some trend among peers, or to look like someone they admire.

Hot Potato

So how do you express yourself? Is it to be uniform with others around you? Or are you being uniform to your beliefs or those of your parents?

Which way is right? It is a difficult question for young people today. It's hard to fight against the crowd, especially when it comes to personal expression.

Hot Potato Questions

- Why do you think young people choose such things as tattooing, body piercing, and fashion to express themselves?
- How do you feel about piercing and tattooing? Is it something you have or would consider acceptable? Why or why not?
- Do you think that these forms of expression ever have a deeper underlying cause? What might that be?
- Can the way you dress, piercings, or tattoos ever affect your chance to get a job? Why might that be? What might be the health risks involved? (Leaders, do your research first. Hepatitis B and C have risen in alarming rates since these behaviors have taken hold of our young people. Skin cancer is associated with both piercings and tattoos. Of course, there are also risks such as infections and allergic reactions. Know the answers to these questions before you present the subject.)
- Do you think these types of choices bring happiness? Why or why not?

Bible Discovery

Genesis 1:27-31. In whose image did God create you? What did He say after creating humanity? Do you think it gives God satisfaction when He sees us living in His image? In what ways does mankind choose not to live in God's image? Are some of the choices we make totally wrong? Can some choices be not so much wrong, but clearly not the best choices we can make? Why or why not? If we are doing our best to live in God's image, can we trust that He will lead us to make the best choices for us?

1 Corinthians 6:19. If we are not our own then that means we were bought with a price. What is that price? How can the choices we make affect the One who paid the price for us? On what basis do you make choices? How can you honor God with "your temple" when you make choices about what to put on or in your body? Is it hard to live in the world and not be a part of it? Especially as a young person? What influences affect how you feel about things such as piercings, fashion, and tattooing? If you make a choice and find out it was the wrong choice, do you believe God can and will forgive you? What if you make a choice that can't be undone physically? Will God look past it to your heart?

Romans 12:1. What does a "spiritual act of worship" mean to you? (Leaders, be ready to lead them in a discussion about this. Things such as going to church when you don't feel like it can be an act of worship.) How do you think the topic we are discussing fits into this? Why? Is it easier to live to please God, or to please your peers? What can you do to live in a way that pleases God? How can you help others battle peer pressure?

Leviticus 19:28. God gave the children of Israel certain specific commands. This is one of them. The reason? Because others around them were getting tattoos and piercings as a form of idol worship, which included worship of their dead. God didn't want the Israelites to be like those around them. People say that things are different today. Do you believe this? Why or why not? Do people still use things such as tattoos, piercings, and fashion to imitate others around them, especially the world? How do you think this verse should fit into a young Christian's life today?

1 Peter 2:12. How does this verse fit in with the previous one? If people think that Christians shouldn't have tattoos or piercings, should we stay away from them so that we don't make others stumble? Is this an easy way to live your life? Who will give you the strength to make the choices you need to make and carry out?

1 Timothy 2:9; 1 Peter 3:3, 4. Where does God say that true beauty comes from? Can you dress in ways that would mask who you are inside? If people see piercings, tattoos, or sloppy and immodest clothing, can they get the wrong picture of who you are? What styles of clothing do you think the Bible would not have us wear? Why? What better ways can we use our money than on expensive clothing and "body jewelry"? Do you believe you are of great worth in God's eyes? Will you trust Him to help you with difficult decisions that might not put you in favor with your peers?

EXTRA GEM

The people of Ellen White's day struggled with keeping up on the world's fashions just as we do today. Read what she wrote: "We cannot afford to live fashionably, for in doing thus, we sacrifice the natural to the artificial. Our artificial habits deprive us of many privileges and much enjoyment, and unfit us for useful life. Fashion subjects us to a hard, thankless life. A vast amount of money is sacrificed to keep pace with changing fashion, merely to create a sensation. The votaries of fashion, who live to attract the admiration of friends and strangers, are not happy—far from it. Their happiness consists in being praised and flattered, and if they are disappointed in this, they are frequently unhappy, gloomy, morose, jealous, and fretful. As a weather vane is turned by the wind, those who consent to live fashionable lives are controlled by every changing fashion, however inconsistent with health and with real beauty" (*Health Reformer*, Oct. 1, 1871).

Sharing Time

It may be hard for you to reach out to others who are struggling with these choices, but do it anyway. God will help you. Make a new friend. Don't criticize or condemn. Learn to be a listener. Sometimes that is all someone really needs—someone to listen and to care. Perhaps then they will want to make different choices.

Consider This

Look into your mirror. What do you see? Do you think you see what God sees? Pray and ask God what needs to be changed about your outward appearance to bring it into line with God's expectations of you. Ask for His help to do this. Then remember that God looks at the inside you—your heart—and that is what He really wants the most!

Ten Commandments
the love of God

This study looks at the Ten Commandments through love and not duty. Prepare by studying and praying for your young people's hearts.

Icebreaker

OK, are you sitting down? Well, sit down! Is there anyone else in the room? You don't want to try this with anyone else watching; they may think you are crazy, and we wouldn't want that to happen!

So sit down and wait for everyone to leave the room. With me? Good.

Now, with your leg hanging down (lying down won't work), lift your right foot off the ground and make clockwise circles in the air. Get them going really good. Now, here's the kicker: take your right hand (don't stop the circles) and at the same time draw the figure of a six in the air.

It happened, didn't it? Your foot reversed directions. Go on. I'll wait while you try it a few dozen more times. Just come back when you're done trying to prove you can do it (or when someone walks into the room). (You can try it on them later.)

Give up? Good. It's just one of those things you have to accept, something in the complicated mass of our brains. Our brains are a complicated system that scientists still haven't completely figured out and probably never will. The brain is the heaviest organ in the body. There are 100 billion neurons in the brain. If you made a stack of 100 billion pieces of paper, it would be about 5,000 miles high, the distance from San Francisco to London.

Dig In

God made our brains truly marvelous. Our brains keep on growing in size until we are about 20 years old, so your brain is still growing. It stores everything that you have seen, heard, felt, touched, and tasted. It is constantly making new connections.

Remember the old adage "You can't teach an old dog new tricks"? Is it true? Most experts would tell you that it isn't true at all. The brain is so amazing that you will have the capacity to learn even if you live to be 100!

Hot Potato

Are you an old dog? Not trying to offend you, but if you are like most people, it is hard to change concepts and ideas once they are learned. What have you been taught about the Ten Commandments? You probably see them as a set of rules that you must follow if you want to please God. You may think of them as a series of "don'ts" that you have no control over. Most think of them as negative and difficult concepts to understand. After all, they were delivered to Moses on a mountain filled with fire and smoke and noise that scared the people enough to ask that God not talk personally to them (see Exodus 20:18-21).

But is that the way God wants us to view the commandments—as a threat? One of the problems people have with the law is thinking it is part of their salvation. That's not the case, and Jesus proved that on the cross. So why do we have the law? Why did God write those words on the stone tablet with His own finger?

The law was nothing new to the children of Israel. The law had been given a long time before they'd even settled in Egypt. It had been given to our first parents—Adam and Eve—in a perfect setting that didn't include sin. What was God's intention in showing His new creation the perfect law? He wanted His children to learn about His character. And what is that character? One word sums it up: *love*. But after sin entered the world, the people began to forget not only God's law but God Himself. So on Sinai, God was just reminding them of His love and His character. And He wants to do the same with us today!

So are you ready to take a new look at something you thought you already knew?

Hot Potato Questions

- Do you think you should be required to keep only the letter of the law?
- Do you think there is a spiritual side of the commandments?
- Which side do you feel we should keep today? Why do you feel this way?

Bible Discovery

Hosea 6:6. Sometimes we make being a Christian too hard. We get caught up in all the rules and worry about everything we say and do. Following the rules is not the same thing as following God. How does God want us to follow Him? Where do we start? Shouldn't following God be something we do with our hearts?

1 Chronicles 29:18, 19. David understood that following God was a heart matter. These verses were a part of a prayer for his son Solomon. Do you think it is what God has in mind for you—to follow Him with your heart? How can you let Him do this in you? What steps do you need to take to open your heart fully to Him?

Deuteronomy 6:5; Mark 12:28-32. When asked what were the greatest of the commandments, what did Jesus say? How did Jesus say that we are to love God? Did He make loving God a heart matter? How can we learn to love those around us? Do we have the ability to do this, or is it something that God gives us the ability to do? What one word sums up what Jesus said is the most important thing about the commandments? Is it love? Is loving always an easy thing? Why or why not?

Exodus 20:1-17. Read the commandments again with your heart open. Can you think of them in a different light knowing that they are given by a loving God? Do the commandments give us a foundation that we can begin to build upon? What do you think our "building" will result in if we let God build His character in us? Is it easier to share a few things we shouldn't do or a whole bunch of things we should do? Do you think that these commandments might be a summary of God's law?

John 15:10. How does Jesus say we can remain in His love? Again, the commandments are tied to the word *love*. Are you beginning to see the character of your Father? Do you think that if He wanted us to stay in His love He would make it difficult to follow His law? Do you think that maybe we, not God, make it difficult?

Revelation 22:13. This is one of the last promises in the Bible. Do you know what alpha and omega are? Alpha is the first letter and omega is the last letter of the classical Greek alphabet. God goes on to explain what He means by saying He is the beginning and the end, the first and the last. If you let God be your beginning and your end—will He also take care of everything else in the middle? Can you trust Him with your life? Do you believe He has the power to help you understand and live His commandments out in your life? Will you let God show you His character and choose to see it with new eyes?

EXTRA GEM

Ellen White was shown how the law was given to Adam and passed down throughout the generations. Read the following quote from *The Faith I Live By*, page 83:

"Adam taught his descendants the law of God, and it was handed down from father to son through successive generations. But . . . there were few who accepted it and rendered obedience. By transgression the world became so vile that it was necessary to cleanse it by the Flood from its corruption. The law was preserved by Noah and his family, and Noah taught his descendants the Ten Commandments. As men again departed from God, the Lord chose Abraham, of whom He declared, 'Abraham obeyed my voice, and kept my charge, my commandments, my statutes, and my laws.' Genesis 26:5."

Sharing Time

Since most people think of the commandments as a negative thing, make it a point this week to share with your friends how you can see God's character in His law and how that character can be summed up with three words: God is love!

Ask God to give you a heart to obey Him and then let others see Him in your life. Remember to serve God out of love, not out of duty.

Consider This

Think about the word "shall." It is the modern form of the word "shalt." It (instead of the word "will") is often used with first-person pronouns (I, we). Now think of it in the second person, "you." You shall. What would that make the commandments? Promises?

What a wonderful way of looking at God's commands! Debbonnaire Kovacs published a terrific book called *God Said "I Promise"* (Pacific Press Publishing Association, 2000) that will help you to look at the commandments in a new light. If you want to learn more, make sure you get a copy and read it!

The Trinity

three in one

As you read through the lesson, remember that the Godhead is one in unity but with three distinct personalities. Each seeks to draw us closer to God. Help the young people understand that unity is the Trinity's desire for us, also. Each of the Trinity has a distinct role that is needed in our lives to draw us to God.

Icebreaker

Water, Water Everywhere

Water. It's everywhere. There are 326 million cubic miles of it on the earth. That's more than 70 percent of the earth's surface. Most of it (97 percent) is salt water that is contained in the oceans. Of the remaining 3 percent, only 0.0002 percent is freshwater that is available for use for agriculture and drinking. The rest is contained in ice caps and glaciers.

In many parts of the world water is in limited supply. There have been many efforts to smarten the use of this essential element. Some of us just love water but waste quite a bit of it. For instance, did you know that every time you flush your toilet an average of five to seven gallons of water is used? And if you like those long, hot showers, you are using, on average, 50 gallons, or about five gallons per minute. If you are one of those people who leave the water on while you brush your teeth, you are using at least three gallons of water that you don't really need.

Conservation is one of the keys to maintaining our freshwater sources. Did you know that if you cut just one minute off your shower time you can save about 150 gallons of water per month? For those who pay for their water, that would make a big difference. Have a dripping faucet? Fix it and save more than 1,200 gallons of water per year.

Why is water important? That big wonderful organ in your skull, the brain, is made up of 85 percent water. Your bones, those things that give your body a frame, are made up of 25 percent water. Water helps your body to regulate its temperature, ensure that food is carried to the organs as needed, and helps get rid of excess salt so it doesn't build up in your body and cause health problems. It also is a component of blood that helps to transport oxygen to your body, and it helps to aid in digestion and elimination. You can live without food for more than a month, but don't try that with water. You can't live a week without the life-giving fluid.

Water has another amazing side: it can be in several forms and still be water. You remember all of this from your science classes. Water can be in liquid form, solid form, and gaseous form, and it is all still water. Amazing!

Dig In

Water—in three forms, but it is still water. Can you think of anything else that might exist in the same way?

Yes: the Godhead—the Father, the Son, the Holy Spirit. It is a difficult concept for us to wrap our minds around. How are the three most important Beings in our lives one, yet individual? All three have a distinct purpose in helping you come to Them. All three love you with an indescribable love. All three have the same plan and purpose for your life. But like water, They all have distinctions that make Them unique and alike at the same time.

Hot Potato

Is It Just a Simple Answer?

Could the explanation of the Trinity be so simple that we just miss it? A look at Matthew 3:16, 17 might help. When Jesus was baptized, what descended from heaven right after He came out of the water? The Holy Spirit. Then a voice was heard. Whose voice was it? God the Father's. So can we conclude from these verses that there are three distinct members of the Godhead, since They all were named? If we go on to look at John 10:30, we see that Jesus says that They are one. It is clear from the Bible that They are individual but that all of Them are God.

Hot Potato Questions

- Is the concept of the Godhead being three yet one hard for you to understand? Why or why not?
- Do you believe that there are three members of the Godhead, each with a distinction? If you try to remove one member, would you still have the Godhead? Why or why not?
- In other religions, why is it so easy to describe their gods and yet different for us? (Leaders, note that in all other religions, the god was made up by humanity. They thought up their ideas and made

them simple to understand. God is not human, so He can't be described in human terms.)

- Are all three members of the Godhead of equal importance? Why or why not?
- If God is beyond human comprehension, then how can we know Him?

Bible Discovery

Genesis 1:26; John 1:1-3. What do these verses have in common? Is it clear from these verses that the Godhead is three separate members with the same purpose and thought? Some churches like to think that Jesus is a created being. Do these verses show that He was there at Creation, helping to form our world? Whose image are we created in?

Matthew 28:16-20. These verses are known as the Great Commission. Did Jesus tell the disciples to go and do the work in His name only? Does the Godhead have the same purpose and plan? Were the things that Jesus commanded us the same as we find in the Old Testament? Does this show that the Godhead has the same purpose and desire, even though They are three separate members?

Deuteronomy 6:4. What does this verse say about the Godhead?

Isaiah 44:8; Romans 1:20-23. These verses talk about God the Father. What attributes of His character do you find in them? Does a person have to have the Bible to know God? Why or why not? Does reading about God help us learn more about Him? Why do you think humanity abandoned the only true God and made for themselves other gods? What is your favorite character trait of your Father? (See also John 1:48.)

Isaiah 9:6; Colossians 1:18-20. For what purposes did God send His Son to earth? What does God's sending His Son for your sins tell you about the characters of both the Father and the Son? Does the name Jesus as described in Isaiah 9:6 show that He too is God? Did Jesus come to show us the character of His Father? Why did He need to do this? What is your favorite character trait of Jesus?

2 Peter 1:21; Acts 1:8; John 14:26; John 16:7-13. According to these verses, list some of the characteristics of the Holy Spirit. Do you see that the Holy Spirit was sent to teach, lead, give us power, and convict us of sin? Did He guide people only from the New Testament? How do you know this? Does He still guide and teach us today? Why is His power to convict of sin so important? What would we do if we didn't have the Spirit to show us the cost of sin and help us turn away from it? What is your favorite character trait of the Holy Spirit?

EXTRA GEM

Ellen White wrote a lot about the ministry of the Godhead. Read what she wrote for us in the following passages:

"We are to cooperate with the three highest powers in heaven—the Father, the Son, and the Holy Ghost—and these powers will work through us, making us workers together with God" (*Evangelism,* p. 617).

"The Comforter that Christ promised to send after He ascended to heaven, is the Spirit in all the fullness of the Godhead, making manifest the power of divine grace to all who receive and believe in Christ as a personal Savior. There are three living persons of the heavenly trio; in the name of these three great powers—the Father, the Son, and the Holy Spirit—those who receive Christ by living faith are baptized, and these powers will cooperate with the obedient subjects of heaven in their efforts to live the new life in Christ" (*ibid.,* p. 615).

Sharing Time

Think of another illustration besides water that might work to describe the Godhead. Use these illustrations to help your friends understand that the Godhead is three individuals, but all one in thought and desire for us. Keep it simple. While it is a concept that is hard to explain, it is also simple at the same time.

Consider This

The Holy Spirit was sent to give us power in what we do for God's kingdom. How often do you ask for this power? This week, remember to ask God to give you the Holy Spirit and His power to work in your life. Keep a journal entry about how things are different for you when you ask for the power God promises.

Types of Entertainment
what are your standards?

Entertainment can be a source of dispute among your young people. Take time to allow them to express their choices in a nonjudgmental way. Plant a seed and let God do the harvesting!

Icebreaker
Move Over, E-mail!
Move over, e-mail. A new cousin is about to take over.

E-mail had its beginnings in the early 1970s, but it wasn't until 1993 that the new technology took off in a big way. The ability to send messages and get replies faster than snail mail changed how the world communicated. E-mail was right for many people—the formality and perfection expected in a written letter couldn't compete with the invention of e-mail. Short notes with quick language became acceptable, and soon everyone had an e-mail address and sometimes more than one!

Fast-forward a few years, the revolution of e-mail has changed more. The advances in new technology have produced a quicker and more fun way to keep in touch! IMing, or instant messaging. There is no cost associated with IMing except for the connection to the Internet. And it doesn't hurt that you can have several windows open at the same time carrying on conversations with multiple people all in almost real time!

Of course, you know all about this, don't you? Young people are IMing kings! Teens beat adults in IMing by leaps and bounds. It has quickly become the preferred method of communication for most teens. Mobile technology allows IMing from cell phones, so no matter where you are, you can be chatting with a friend using IMing technology.

Although most young people use IMing to chat with friends, they use it for other reasons as well. Almost half of teens admit they use it for discussions they prefer not to have in person. Awkward situations are more easily discussed when we don't have to do it face to face—things such as asking for a date, or breaking up, avoiding potential embarrassment.

Many young people use it while they are doing other things, such as studying. So when you do your research for your next big school project, remember: technology may exist, but it is up to you to choose to use it wisely.

Dig In

Technology is growing daily. As soon as you buy the latest gadget and walk out the door with it, something new is about to come on the market. The choices young people have for entertainment have grown along with advances in technology. Many choices of entertainment, whether in music, TV, video gaming, or movies, didn't exist just a few decades ago. And with these overwhelming advances comes responsibility for the choices you make.

Hot Potato

Is the Price Right?

If something is available, does that make it right for you? This is a tough question with even tougher choices you have to make in your life. There is very little that isn't available to savvy, technologically minded young people.

Pac-Man was one of the first video games to become widely available. Chasing the snapping character around a maze took up many hours of people's time. Now turn on your gaming console, and you can put yourself in action, with almost 3-D-like effects. The availability of free downloads of music and iPods makes listening to your favorite musicians easy and portable. Cable television opens the movie industry up to even nontheatergoers.

So what is the price of all this new technology?

Hot Potato Questions

- How does advancing technology affect your entertainment choices?
- What responsibilities do you think Christians have when making entertainment choices?
- Are there video games that you feel a Christian young person should not play? Which ones and why?
- Do you think entertainment is an individual's choice?
- Can one game or movie or type of music be right for one Christian

young person but not for another? Why do you feel this way?

- What rating for movies is beyond what you choose to watch? Do you make these choices yourself, or are you guided by your parents?
- Do you feel that all music labeled "Christian" is acceptable to listen to? Why or why not?
- What guides how you use your free time? Can you make good choices in entertainment bad by using your time unwisely? How?
- How do you think God feels about the choices of entertainment you make?
- Is there room for improvement in how you use your time?
- Can you be a Christian and still have fun?

Bible Discovery

Proverbs 17:22. Do you think God wants you to be happy? Modern research has shown that laughter is good medicine. Can you make choices of entertainment that are fun and still glorify your Father? Why or why not? Do you make these kinds of choices? Is anything keeping you from using your downtime wisely? What? How can you change this?

Matthew 25:21. How much of your time is truly "your time"? Does God require us to be faithful in just the large things He gives to us, or do the little things matter too? If you are faithful with your time, will God give you even better things to do? Do you see God as happy? Why or why not? Was Jesus happy when He was on the earth? Point out specific examples for what you believe.

John 2:1-11. Jesus' first miracle was at a wedding. Who was there with Him? What do you think Jesus was showing us by His example? Do you think that Jesus and His disciples laughed and had fun? Why or why not? Is that a hard image for you to imagine? Is God social? If He is, do you think it is a desire that He built in us? Can celebrating help us see the beauty and meaning in life? Are there good and bad forms of social behavior? List a few bad forms and a few good forms of social behavior. Where do your personal choices fit in with these?

Proverbs 5:22. How can the choices you make about entertainment "ensnare" (NIV) you? Are certain behaviors addictive? Do some of the new technologies come with new temptations? How do you handle these? What are some good ways you can talk with your friends to help them deal with the temptations that technology brings? Does God understand temptation? Does He forgive wrong choices if we ask Him to? What is our responsibility when we ask for forgiveness?

Romans 12:1, 2. In using new technologies and choices of entertainment, are you conforming to the standards of the world? Why or why not? How can we be separate from the world and yet reach out to others? What do you think "living sacrifice" means? Does it mean that you have to give up having fun with your friends? Why or why not? Can choices of entertainment lead us away from God? If you ask, will God lead you in all the choices in your life? Are you at a point in your life where you want God to help you with your choices?

EXTRA GEM

Ellen White was shown how distracting the things of this world can be, and what they can be used for. Read what she wrote:

"The lust of the eye, the desire for excitement and pleasing entertainment, is a temptation and snare to God's people. Satan has many finely woven, dangerous nets which are made to appear innocent, but with which he is skillfully preparing to infatuate God's people. There are pleasing shows, entertainments, phrenological lectures, and an endless variety of enterprises constantly arising calculated to lead the people of God to love the world and the things that are in the world" (*Testimonies*, vol. 1, p. 550).

Sharing Time

Plan a party with your youth group or other Christian friends. Think about good choices you can make that will entertain them and also let them know about God's character. Take time with your planning and make it a great event. Have fun! You'll show yourself and your friends that being a Christian doesn't mean that you can't be happy and have fun!

Consider This

Make a list of the things you do in your spare time. Which of these do you think are good choices? Which might need some help? Pray over your list and ask God to help you make wise choices. Adjust your list as God leads you.

Unity
the body of Christ

As you prepare for this lesson, help the young people understand that unity does not mean giving up our individual personalities. Like the Godhead, unity of purpose is God's desire for us and keeps us in His will, where it is safest to be. Young people sometimes have an easier grasp of unity than adults.

Icebreaker
The President Gets Dirty

He was a United States president. Yet there he stood among the other laborers building a home for low-income residents. He wasn't there just for publicity. Wearing faded jeans and a flannel shirt, he had a hammer in his hands and knew how to use it. His wife—a bandanna wrapped around her hair—worked nearby. Their hands were dirty and calloused from the work. The year was 1984, and the former thirty-ninth president was in New York putting up walls for what would be an affordable home for a needy family. The Carters continue that work today. In November 2009 President Carter and his wife joined thousands of volunteers for a weeklong build-off in some of the poorest areas of Asia to construct homes for more than 300 families—many living on less than US$1 a day.

Habitat for Humanity is the organization President Carter and his wife, Rosalynn, are working with. Started in 1976 by Millard and Linda Fuller, the international organization helps families in need of housing by building affordable homes at low cost with many hours of volunteer labor. The families are not given a complete freebie. They purchase the homes at no interest and donate many hours of labor toward them, or that of another family in need, something Habitat calls "sweat equity." Sometimes the homes take weeks to build, and sometimes "blitzes" are accomplished, whereby a home can be completed in 24 hours. One thing is certain—whatever country the homes are built in, they are safe, secure, and well built, often far superior to other homes in the area.

One of the greatest assets of Habitat for Humanity International is its volunteers. People from all over the world join with others to build these homes. The unity and purpose of the volunteers is amazing. In its years of service, Habitat for Humanity International has built an astounding 500,000 houses, making a new home a reality for more than 2.5 million people in more than 3,000 communities worldwide—all with volunteer hours and donated materials.

It's amazing what can be accomplished when people work together to do something—and they are united in purpose and desire. There is tremendous power in unity.

Dig In

Unity should be a concept we understand well. After all, Jesus talked about it often in the Bible, urging His followers to have nothing else but complete unity. Did they? Yes, for the most part. There were some noted disagreements as they struggled to bring individual personalities and wills into line with God's will. And when they got it right, big things happened. The church grew daily! Not just a baptism here or there after an evangelistic campaign, but daily! They worked together—pooling their resources— and everyone's needs were met.

Fast-forward to today. Is there unity in your church? your Sabbath school class? your home? We may strive for unity, but too many are not reaching that goal.

Why?

Hot Potato

A Battle of Wills?

One of the main reasons we don't achieve unity is that we battle over wills. We want our will, and want others to agree with it! But that is not what unity is. It isn't pulling together and agreeing to disagree amicably. It isn't trying to agree for the most part. It's giving up our wills for the will of God. We will never get there by minimizing differences and maximizing similarities. The only way we will find unity is to obey God's will. That truth is found in His Word. The treasures we need to seek are found between the covers of the Bible.

We need to work together as one body, just as in 1 Corinthians 12. There Paul says that the body (the church) is made up of many different parts, but it is all the same body. Each part is important and needed, and no part is better than another. After explaining how the church should act like a body, he goes on in the next chapter to share the secret of how all of this unity can take place—through love, God's perfect love! We just need to listen.

Hot Potato Questions

- Is the unity Jesus spoke of in the Bible possible in today's world given the diversity of faiths? Why do you feel that way?
- Can Christians from different churches find a place of unity?
- Is God calling us to have unity of doctrine or unity of faith? Is there a difference?
- Why is it hard to give up your will and accept God's will?
- Can you do anything to allow that change in your life?
- What things keep your church from finding complete unity? What problems cause these disagreements?
- Can you do anything to help others see that they need unity in Jesus?
- Is everyone in your church made to feel a part of the church? Why or why not?
- In what ways do you want to have unity in your life?

Bible Discovery

John 17:23. In this verse we see Jesus' prayer to His Father. In it, He prays for Himself, His disciples, and all believers to come. In verses 20 to 23 especially, He prays that believers to come would find unity. There are two things that He says will happen as a result of this unity. What are they? (Leaders, Jesus says that the world will know that He is the Son of God sent by God, and that we would know the Father's love.) Jesus makes a remarkable statement here. He says that God loves us as He loves Jesus. Have you ever thought of that? Do you believe God loves you as much as He loves Jesus? Why or why not? It is almost overwhelming when we realize the magnitude of God's love. If He loves you that much, how can you ever look at someone else the same way? Does it make you see that everyone is loved by God and that you need to love them, too? Is that easy to do? If we can get to that point—will unity be more possible?

Ephesians 4:1-6. In what ways do these verses describe how our actions should be toward one another? Did Jesus demonstrate these attitudes when He was on the earth? Do these attitudes come naturally? How can we achieve these in our lives? Will putting others ahead of ourselves help us to be more like Jesus asks us to be? Does God exercise patience with you? Should you be more patient with others?

Colossians 3:16. What do you think is the message that Paul talks about in this verse? How can we teach and "admonish" one another if we don't love? Will teaching without love and patience be successful? Why or why not? What other ways were the believers to encourage one another? How can singing songs of praise encourage unity? Is music a universal language among Christians? Why or why not?

Acts 4:32-35. In what two ways does it say the believers were united? Do you feel that you are united in mind and heart with others in your group? Should you be? What keeps us from achieving this? The believers at that time shared their common good with one another. Today we live more separate lives. Do we still have an obligation to help others when we can? Does helping someone make you feel closer to them? Do you think that might be what God wants you to learn, to care for others instead of caring only for your needs? As a young person without a lot of income, how can you model this behavior in your life?

2 Corinthians 5:17-21. Could the secret to unity lie in becoming a new creation in Christ? Will God faithfully help you to become the person He means for you to be? Do you have to let Him? Will this transformation help us to want to reach out to others and share the good news of Jesus? Ambassadors are more than just messengers; they are representatives of the sovereign that sent them. In our case, we are representatives of the King of the universe! Can we do this under our own strength? Can remembering whom we represent help us to work toward the unity God calls us to?

EXTRA GEM

Even in Ellen White's day, there was a lack of unity in the church. The battle of wills has been in humanity since the beginning. Read what she writes can happen if we seek unity: "The success of our work depends upon our love to God and our love to our fellowmen. When there is harmonious action among the individual members of the church, when there is love and confidence manifested by brother to brother, there will be proportionate force and power in our work for the salvation of men. Oh, how greatly we need a moral renovation! Without the faith that works by love, you can do nothing. May the Lord give you hearts to receive this testimony" (*Testimonies to Ministers,* p. 188).

Sharing Time

Unity comes when we learn to love as God wants. What ways can you personally seek to help others and demonstrate the attitude God wants in His children? Pick someone you know needs to feel more loved in your church and reach out to them. Ask if you can have this person over for Sabbath dinner, sit by them in church, write a note to encourage them. Write a small note to thank them for something they do that goes unnoticed, even if it is just their great smile. It will encourage them and you will be blessed, too!

Consider This

Reread 1 Corinthians 13. Write out the things that love is and isn't. Then look over the list and see areas that you need to let the Spirit work with you on. Pray over your list and open your heart to God and see what marvelous things He will do in your life!

Values and Standards
where do they come from?

Young people are just learning to make their standards and values their own. Influences of the world are so strong at this age. Encourage them to use God's Word for their choice of standards to help them become all they can be.

Icebreaker

Rising Above the Tide

All work stops. Everyone's attention is drawn to the man at the center of the village.

He is accused of acting irresponsibly. One by one, every man, woman, and child walks slowly to form a circle around this one who has committed the crime. All faces search his eyes—wondering what they will find there. He stands alone, in the center of the village, guilty. He knows it and knows what he deserves. They know it too.

This is the Babemba tribe of South Africa. And what is about to happen will astound you. This man, guilty of injustice, will be treated very differently than you would expect.

The tribe—every member of it—has formed a circle around the man. And instead of hurling accusations or stones, they instead treat him with love. Each member, from the youngest to the oldest, takes the time to remind the violator of his good qualities. They search their memories for all the good times spent together. They recall good deeds that the person has done. They remember kindnesses shown. Every positive affirmation they can think of is shared with this member of their family. They remind him of their love for him. The ceremony, often lasting days, is never hurried or cut short. Every member of the tribe has something to add, and all wait in patience as this is done.

When the circle is finally broken, the offending member, newly forgiven, is symbolically welcomed back into the tribe and greeted with joyful celebration. The offender is healed, and so is the village.

This Babemba tribe, found in the republic of Zambia, has passed on a legacy of love to their members, something that sets them apart in how they value each member of their tribal family. What a lesson we can learn from their example.

Dig In

Our values and standards are important in our lives. They are part of our belief system. They affect how we do what we do and how we think. They affect how we treat others and what we expect from them. In fact, our standards and values are an important part of who we are.

So what do you value most? It's a question we don't often stop to think about, but we should. Getting our values in order helps us focus on what is most important in our lives. The clearer you are about what you believe in and why, the more effective you will be in life and the more happiness you will receive.

Mark Twain once wrote, "If you think you can, you can. If you think you can't, you're right." Somehow, you need to know what you believe in and put your values in order. Then there will be little stopping you!

Hot Potato

From Big Screen to Small Screen

Where do your standards and values come from? As Christians, this is a very important question because the world is watching us. Like it or not, we are to set a higher standard than the world. Our lives are examples of our heavenly Father, and we are to be a light in the world. If you claim the name Christian, then you must be an example of the One who makes you a Christian. It doesn't mean that you won't fail sometimes, but the world is watching and what they see will influence their decision in who/what they choose to follow.

It's not easy living in a fishbowl, but it comes with the choice of being one of God's children.

Now that you are maturing, you will begin to set up your own system of standards and values. We initially get them from many places. First and foremost, our values come from our parents. They teach us what they believe and place value on, and that gets passed down to you. We get our standards from church. We watch others and learn from their lives. We get our ideas on living from God's Word. It is the ultimate book on living right. Our culture also affects how we live.

But there are other influences, too, that make up who we are and what we value. Like it or not, Hollywood has a big influence on us. And many of those values have jumped from the big screen to the small screen—television. Much of what we value is taken from what we see—and for many, that means television. The media influences us greatly. But it is our choice to let this happen.

So how do you make your values your own and not your parents'? How do you choose whom to follow and what standards to live by?

Hot Potato Questions

- If you take a look at your life, can you clearly see what values and standards are most important to you?
- If not, how will you be able to define your values?
- Can you look at your friends and see your values through their lives? Do the people you admire help to define your values?
- How about the material you read? Does it set a standard for your life? Is that standard one that you want to continue?
- Does the type of music and other entertainment you enjoy reflect your standards and values?
- Do you think you are called to be an example to others? Why or why not?
- Have you allowed the standards and values of the world to creep into your life? Are your values based on opinions? Should they be based on the Word of God?
- Is your life example consistent with what you think your values are? If not, what do you need to do about it?

Bible Discovery

Romans 12:2. Why do you think the Bible says that we shouldn't look to the world for our standards and values? What values would we most likely find there? Are there any good things in the world around us that we can emulate? Where does good come from? Is it in humanity's nature to do good? Why or why not? Where can we find the best place to secure our values? How can we be transformed? Is it hard work? Is it worth the price?

Matthew 5:16. Do you sometimes feel that you are living in a fishbowl? Should you live that way? Does what others think about you make a difference? Should the way you dress and the way you behave always set an example of who you are inside? Why or why not? Can the way you dress and act change others' perception of you in a way that you don't want them to? How can you "let your light shine" without seeming that you are trying to be too good? Should that matter? Why or why not? Do people in the world want to have a good example to follow?

1 Peter 2:12. Is it hard work to always live right? Why or why not? What happens when we make a mistake? Will others' perceptions of us change? Will God forgive us when we slip? Does living right give you a guarantee that life will be easy and perfect? Why or why not? If we are accused of doing wrong when we are living right, who will be our judge? Does your age give you an excuse for your behavior? Why do you think that way? Do adults expect young people to live right? Can you, at a young age, be a powerful witness to others by your behavior and choices?

1 Corinthians 3. What foundation does Paul encourage us to build on? When is that foundation laid in our lives? Does Paul encourage the people to look to him or Apollos as an example? Are we called to be farmers—to make ready the soil, plant it, and gather the harvest? What are we called to do? Is a seed planter also a harvester? How can you plant good seeds with your life example? Does planting always mean a good harvest? Do you need to examine your values and standards and see if they are what you truly want them to be?

EXTRA GEM

Ellen White wrote about values that come from the world. Read what she wrote: "We are Christ's witnesses, and we are not to allow worldly interests so to absorb our time and attention that we pay no heed to the things that God has said must come first. There are higher interests at stake. 'Seek ye first the kingdom of God and His righteousness.' Christ gave His all to the work that He came to do, and His word to us is, 'If any man will come after Me, let him deny himself, and take up his cross, and follow Me.' 'So shall ye be My disciples.' Willingly and cheerfully Christ gave Himself to the carrying out of the will of God. He became obedient unto death, even the death of the cross. Shall we feel it a hardship to deny ourselves? Shall we draw back from being partakers of His sufferings? His death ought to stir every fiber of the being, making us willing to consecrate to His work all that we have and are. As we think of what He has done for us, our hearts should be filled with love" (*Messages to Young People,* p. 314).

Sharing Time

How can you set a standard that others would want to adopt? Think about the way you dress, your entertainment choices, and how you talk. Are they showing your inner values? What can you do to influence others to make good choices? Brainstorm and make a list of the qualities you most admire. Then make a list of the qualities you should most admire. Are they the same? What do you need to do about it?

Consider This

Make a top 10 list of the values you want in your life. Order them in importance from the most valuable to the least valuable. Now look at the list. Where do your top values come from? Are they yours or someone else's? What can you do to make your values your own? Ask God for help. He values you more than anything.

Why I Go to Church
Jesus' example of fellowship

Leaders, study this lesson before you present it. You will be helping the young people understand why God wants us to attend church. Make sure that you can explain to them why you choose to attend church. You can be sure they will listen to your example. Be honest; young people value honesty.

Icebreaker
The Safest Place to Be!

Church is the safest place to be! Did you know that? You should avoid riding in automobiles, because they're responsible for 20 percent of all fatal accidents. You really shouldn't stay at home, though, because 17 percent of all accidents happen in the home. Whatever you do, avoid walking on the street or sidewalks, because 14 percent of all accidents occur to pedestrians. And of course, never travel by air, rail, or water, because 16 percent of all accidents involve these forms of transportation. Are you adding statistics up? It leaves 33 percent. Of those, 32 percent of all deaths occur in the hospital, so whatever you do, don't go to a hospital.

Now you are left with just 1 percent. So where is the safest place to be? You'll be happy to know that only .001 percent of all deaths occur in church! And these are usually related to a preexisting condition. So church really is the safest place to be. And here's one more safe thing—Bible study. The percentage of deaths occurring during Bible studies is even less than the others.

Of course, there is no way to avoid doing most of the above, but it makes a great point, huh? Church is a safe place to be for many reasons, but some people rely too much on that safety. Are you one of them?

Dig In

So why go to church? Have you ever asked yourself that question? Did you start going with your parents so it's become a habit? And if it is a good habit, does that make it right for you?

Going to church used to be a family ritual. The family is the basic unit of any society. When the family unit was strong, the church was strong and people attended together. But what is happening to the family unit? The answer to that question is quite clear. The family unit is breaking down and changing into something very different than in times past. A two-parent family with children is not the norm any longer. Single parents, blended families, generations living together are the more normal family of today's world. Loving God and attending church usually comes from the family first. Where does today's family fit in to this?

Hot Potato
Attend With the Hypocrites?

Some people say they don't like going to church because of the hypocrisy. Does it discourage you when you see people in high positions abuse their power? How do you handle people who profess what they don't possess? How about when someone talks about something that they believe isn't right but later in the week you see them doing that very thing? Has that ever happened to you? How do you handle the examples modeled for you? Perhaps you have been hurt by someone in the church through a careless remark or a painful encounter. Can you get past it to truly worship God? What's wrong with just staying home? What about just maybe watching a religious program on television?

We can make lots of excuses for all kinds of behavior. We are human, and humans love to make excuses. It is easy to do, isn't it? When we feel hurt, or unwanted, or disappointed in someone else, it is easy to make an excuse not to go to church. Remember, it is easy to follow anything when it is convenient. It's when things get tough that it becomes more difficult to choose to follow.

So where do we look for an example? Jesus. He is the only safe place to keep our eyes focused. Now, ask yourself, Did Jesus go to church with a bunch of hypocrites? Got your answer yet? Let's name a few: the Pharisees, the Sadducees, the chief priests, the Sanhedrin. Is that enough? All of them had some guilt in His crucifixion, but the Bible tells us that Jesus was in church on the Sabbath day (see Luke 4:16). Jesus had the best excuse of all not to go to church—He was God! Yet we read that He went regularly. Do we need a better example?

Hot Potato Questions
- Do you ever feel that not attending church is better for your spiritual life than attending?

- Do you ever leave church more discouraged than when you went?
- When you feel this way, can going to church become a "spiritual act of worship," something you do for God and not for yourself?

Bible Discovery

Romans 3:23. How many people in the church are sinners? Has there ever been any individual on earth besides Jesus who has not sinned? Will there ever be a sinless individual (except for Jesus)? How does that help us see the church? Is it truly a hospital for sinners, or a haven for saints?

John 3:16, 17. Why did God send His Son, Jesus, into the sinful world? Does that include you? Does God want to condemn us? How does the Bible tell us we can inherit eternal life? Can we gain eternal life by going to church? Does the church have power to save anyone? Then why do you think we go to church? People often misunderstand that the act of going to church is not what will change us. It is the encounter we have with God that will make us into better people. Worshipping God can and will change us.

Hebrews 10:24, 25. Does the Bible encourage us to meet or go to church? The early Christians were already developing some habits that Paul wrote about in Hebrews. He told them to encourage one another and to meet regularly. He also told them something else. He told them to spur one another on toward love and good deeds. Can attending church help us to do that? By discussing God's Word with others, can we learn new insights? Can we see things through different eyes? Does meeting together regularly make us more of a family? Do families sometimes disagree? Since all have sinned, including those in the church, can we reasonably expect that there will be some hypocrisy in the church? Can attending church help you grow in the Lord? Does it ever do the opposite? When does the Bible tell us that we should especially be careful and meet together? Will the support of others help you if you are alive just before Christ comes?

Matthew 24:50, 51. Who has the power to judge the hypocrisy that is so prevalent today? Where does the Bible say that the bad servant will be assigned a place? Can we then leave the judgment of hypocrites to God? Can you trust Him to take care of those who discourage your faith? In His love, would He rather help them overcome their hypocrisy or condemn them? (Remember John 3:16, 17.)

Matthew 7:7. What does the Bible say about how we can gain knowledge of Jesus and His saving grace? Is this a promise that you can count on? God clearly wants us to ask, seek, and knock. Can attending church help us see things that we can investigate further in God's Word?

1 John 1:3, 4. John wanted to encourage believers who were being misguided by false teachers in the church. The word for fellowship here is the Greek word for partnership. Do you think that God wants us to have a partnership with Him? How about with other believers? Where can you grow the fastest—on your own, or with others who believe as you do?

EXTRA GEM

Read this quote from Ellen White and be encouraged. God needs you! "The church is languishing for the help of young men who will bear a courageous testimony, who will with their ardent zeal stir up the sluggish energies of God's people, and so increase the power of the church in the world" (*Messages to Young People*, p. 24).

Sharing Time

Look up Proverbs 27:17. What does it tell you that fellowship with other believers can do in your life? Think of someone you know who needs the good news of God's saving grace and the fellowship that is gained by worshipping God with others. Make a definite plan to invite them to a special youth time at your church. Also, find someone whom you can share the study of God's Word with. You won't just be encouraging yourself; you'll be encouraging other seekers.

Consider This

Do you have a hard time concentrating in church sometimes? Use these steps to help refresh your worship. 1. Ready your mind. You will get out of your worship experience what you put in. 2. Take notes. It will help you focus and concentrate on what is being said and also give you notes to look back on when sharing with others. 3. Get involved. Feeling needed will help you focus on feeling a part of the group!

DO GOD AND CHURCH REALLY MATTER?

We don't always feel a need for God—unless we've hit rock bottom. But even if you're well off, well fed, and well educated, life truly is better with God. Nathan Brown considers seven reasons God matters in everyday life, revealing that whether things are good or bad, God makes them better still. 978-0-8127-0436-5. Paperback, 160 pages.

3 WAYS TO SHOP

- **Visit your local Adventist Book Center®**
- **Call toll-free 1-800-765-6955**
- **Online at AdventistBookCenter.com**
  Availability subject to change.

REVIEW AND HERALD®
PUBLISHING ASSOCIATION
Since 1861 | www.reviewandherald.com

Ready For An Authentic Change?

Authentic
Scott R. Ward

If you've ever wanted a genuine, thriving relationship with Jesus but didn't know exactly what to do to make it happen, this book was written for you. Even if going through the motions has left you empty, if reading the Bible and praying are just two extra items on your daily to-do list, if you feel far from God, there is hope.

Within these pages you'll discover how to come heart to heart with Jesus in Scripture, what role multisensory symbols have in the devotional experience, and the key elements of a mutually satisfying, lifelong journey with Jesus. 978-0-8280-2623-1

SHOP YOUR WAY
» **Visit** your local Adventist Book Center
» **Call** toll-free 800.765.6955
» **Click** www.AdventistBookCenter.com

 Review&Herald.

REVIEW AND HERALD® PUBLISHING ASSOCIATION | SINCE 1861 | WWW.REVIEWANDHERALD.COM

Whose side are you on, anyway?

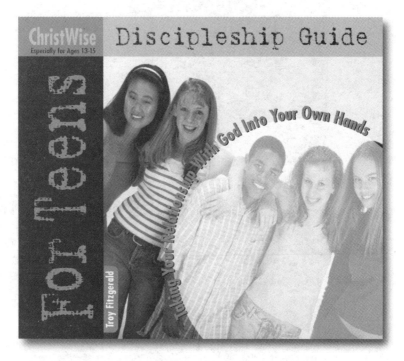

I t's the most important decision you'll ever make! This discipleship guide will not only show you how to be a follower of Christ, but also teach you how to become a peer mentor! More than just a baptismal course, this is an exciting way to begin a new life. 0-8280-1711-5. Paperback, 128 pages.

3 WAYS TO SHOP

- **• Visit your local Adventist Book Center®**
- **• Call toll-free 1-800-765-6955**
- **• Online at AdventistBookCenter.com**
  Availability subject to change.

REVIEW AND HERALD®
PUBLISHING ASSOCIATION
Since 1861 | www.reviewandherald.com